Psalms Of Praises

to the gospel of saint john

Psalms Of Praises

to the gospel of saint john

Rick Hohn

Printed in the United States of America

Publishing services by Selah Publishing Group, LLC, Indiana. The views expressed or implied in this work do not necessarily reflect those of Selah Publishing Group.

ISBN: 1-58930-139-0
Library of Congress Control Number: 2004097052

DEDICATION

All praise and thanks go to the Holy Spirit, who is the true author of this devotional book to glorify God the Father, and the Lord Jesus Christ. It truly was His Spirit working in me as I wrote only three words at a time. I had no preconceived notion of what to say next, yet I know that the Spirit gave me these words of praise.

My undying gratitude extends to the members of my church home fellowship that motivated and encouraged me to have <u>Psalms of Praises</u> published, after lying dormant for more than 20 years.

I would like to thank Bob Fulton along with Verge and Audrey Ford, who corrected the typos in my manuscript. Also, I can't forget to express my thanksgiving to Rose Biller, who originally transferred the type written text to her computer years ago. Little did she know that Bob would ask her this spring for help in changing the format from poetry to prose.

Finally, I thank all of my friends that made the publication of this praise devotional book possible through their financial contributions.

May God bless each one of you,

– Rick Hohn

FOREWORD

Psalms of Praises from a life of Praise, Rick Hohn's life is a praise every day. I am so honored to have been asked to write the foreword for this lovely Meditation. Rick's words come from a heart of love and adoration that is beyond what most of us will ever know.

The words, phrases and sentences are poetry for the soul. The last sentence of the book says it all. "My praise is like a mist of what You truly deserve!"

I can say with longing that I wish I could speak with such eloquence to my Lord. What a balm Rick's thoughts must be to Him...who has to put up with children who might blow Him a quick kiss as we run about trying to "do" the next good thing on our agenda ...for Him.

Rick is God's choice Child. Think with me for a moment. You or I can input our thoughts quickly into the computer, our fingers keeping up with our thoughts. We can think a word and type it out instantly... Yet most of us never do it. Rick thinks in his mind a beautiful sentence...and it takes him thirty to forty-five minutes to laborious type out that one sentence with a stylus on his head. There is no way that I could keep a sentence in my head for that long....yet, thought after thought, page after page, hour after hour, God has a child who can and WILL focus on Him.

– Mary Francess Froese

PREFACE

Praise God for How He Made Me

"There is Power in praise! Your autobiography will follow", was what several friends of my church home fellowship shouted after I asked them to pray about which book to get published first. Accolades from heaven witnessed this to my heart – knowing that the Lord wanted me finally to get <u>Psalms of Praises to the Gospel of Saint John</u>, which I wrote 20 years ago, out to the lovers of our Lord Jesus Christ.

To give the <u>Psalms of Praises to The Gospel of Saint John</u> a more personal impact, this preface about me will enable you, the reader, to witness how the Holy Spirit can use someone in spite of a disability, in my case, cerebral palsy. This statement is certainly not to engender pity or to bring myself glory, but that you would see how God's strength is perfected in weakness - (2nd Corinthians 12:9). For in me, the Lord has done an amazing work.

You will probably be surprised if we should meet. Twenty years ago, I was shocked when a friend asked me to look at myself in a full-length mirror (probably an exercise in self-esteem). This was my first gaze in a mirror since childhood in physical therapy.

In looking at myself in the mirror at 36 years of age, I was quite taken back. The degree of damage to my brain's motor section had quite an effect on my appearance. My arms and legs looked abnormally thin and disproportionate to my head. To keep involuntary movements to a minimum, my right leg was crossed over my left and under again — creating a doubling affect. My right arm was pinned between my legs, and my left arm was strapped tightly in the wheelchair's seatbelt.

Old-fashioned, brown-framed eyeglasses were tied with a bright red elastic band around my head. The red band was so that my glasses wouldn't fall off when I bent down or shook my balding head, which was uncombed from being out in the wind. For communication purposes, I had a headband made in part from a welding hat with a pointer attached to it.

I said to myself, "What a freak! Is that really me? No wonder that kids have come up to me and asked if I'm from Mars! Some of the nurses in the convalescent hospital treat me like dirt. They can't stand the sight of me!"

My friend, sensing my low self-esteem, ministered to me. She reassured me that God created me this way and that I am beautiful in His sight. She asked me to name just one thing that I liked about myself. I took another embarrassing glance at myself in the mirror. I hated what I saw - my skinny, under-developed body, my toothpick arms and legs twisted beyond normal proportions, my buckteeth, the foreign headband gadget, my weird-looking glasses and my eyes that were filled with shock and embarrassment.

Slowly, my eyes began to sparkle, though. The more I looked the more they sparkled, resulting unexpectedly in a glowing smile. I saw the glory of God in my own eyes - much like the radiant eyes of an expectant mother.

The eyes are the windows to the soul. This is especially true in my case. Look in my eyes; you will see our Lord's Joy, Love, Peace, and Warmth. Look in my eyes while I am singing worship songs, though my speech is garbled. My voice is weird and choppy, but still I love to sing. I can't understand people who possess a normal voice and say that they can't sing. Though it is a struggle, I attempt to raise my right hand when praising the Lord. He is worthy of all my praise that I can give. And on occasions, I love to dance in the spirit from my wheelchair.

In this environment, you will see the results of a purely enthusiastic appreciation and utter joy over my personal, intimate relationship with the Lord Jesus.

In describing myself, I mentioned a headband with a pointer that I wear. When I was 15 years old, my dad invented this apparatus that opened doors for me to write by pressing keys on an electric typewriter (now a computer). Naturally, this was a very slow process - taking an entire day to complete one poem - but it is all worthwhile. With the head stylus, I also learned to flip pages of a book, turn my stereo on and off, dial my push button speakerphone, and access a speaking device, which I now deliver sermons and national presentations. Additionally, I can attach a paintbrush to my pointer and do oil paintings that I sell.

I first began writing poems to the Lord in 1981 when Ralph Moore, the Founding Pastor of Hope Chapel in Hermosa Beach, California, challenged the congregation to find new forms of worship on an individual basis. One night I was depressed and discouraged about my powered wheelchair not being fixed after a year. The spokes of my manual chair were starting to break, making it next to impossible to get around the big 200 bed convalescent hospital at the time. The nurses seemed too busy to care about my plight. I was still recovering from the heartache of a divorce and felt even more discouraged when the church van failed to show up for the third Sunday in a row. One of the things that I enjoy is worshipping and praising God. So missing Sunday night services when the Holy Spirit was most present was extremely disappointing, and I felt crushed when the van driver forgot to pick us up.

I remember the pastor's words of encouragement to find new forms of worship. I had in mind to write a letter to Jesus or write something on my electric IBM typewriter as my new form of worship. With my right foot, I struggled to push myself backwards in my broken-down manual chair down the block-long hallway to my room so that I could type. I started to write a few words that I felt the Holy Spirit was giving me about my helpless predicament, and about how much greater God was to satisfy my needs. By the end of the poem, I was so excited from a spirit of joy welling up in me that I found it hard to go to bed when the nurses were ready to put me in bed. Writing the poem of praise was greater than attending the Sunday night worship service. I thanked God that the driver forgot to pick us up. It was a new experience in writing. I always had preconceived thoughts about content, but this time I had no foreknowledge of the finished product - the Holy Spirit gave me only a few words at a time. In addition, I had no experience as a poet; still the Lord led me through it in the manner of the Old Testament psalmist. It was truly amazing.

I shared my poems with a home fellowship from church, and through them the Lord was able to minister to the members. Everybody encouraged me to do more poems of praise. Over the course of the next two years, I kept writing and it continued to lift my spirits up in worship and praise to God, and it blessed others as I shared with them. Often I have left a poem with a tip for waitresses, and the response has been good.

Since these poems ministered both to me as a writer and to my readers, I decided to undertake the writing of praises as I go through the Gospel of Saint John. Admittedly, my intentions were primarily less than Bible study but were to give inspiration as the Spirit leads.

Read Psalms of Praises as a daily devotional after reviewing the selected scriptures from John's Gospel. Although it was written 20 years ago, it is fresh and alive like it was written today. It is my prayer that from this encounter with the Holy Spirit, additional praises would well inside of you and flow from you as they are either spoken or written. When noted as a "Personal Testimony", I give insights of experiences in my life so that the Bible would become more real. I pray that you will be as blessed from the reading of it.

chapter one

Praise God for Who He is

JOHN 1:1-5

PRAISE FOR THE ETERNAL GOD

You are worthy and to be praised, my Eternal God and Lord, pre-existing all Your Creation! Father, with Jesus Your Son, before the beginning, You formed everything and more than my eye can see. Being the Creator, you sustain life; You hold the universe in your hand.

O Lord, my God, You make my heart secure whenever I ponder and meditate that You existed before the first atom and that You had no beginning! You are eternal - as far as the east from the west and you are not bound by time for a thousand years are unto you as one day. I give praise to You, Jesus, for you did not come to be at the first Christmas two thousand years ago, but You, the Word of God, created all things-the Mountains, the valleys, and the stars! You made all things beautiful to your glory, and made me to dwell in and share this glory! When I go astray,

You restore me to walk in the light again with You! Lord, I cannot fathom with my natural mind how you existed without birth, how you created everything so beautifully and perfectly, and how privileged I am to even live in the midst of such beauty! Praise you, Jesus, for being my light, to understand this mystery, and to comprehend through eyes of faith the wonders of your greatness!

JOHN 1:6-13

PRAISE GOD FOR HIS LIGHT IN ME
(PERSONAL TESTIMONY)

I give thanksgiving to You, O Lord, for revealing Your glorious Light through others in my life just as John the Baptist bore witness to Your Light. Thank You for Your shining Light through my mother who first told me about You, Jesus, about Your great Love and how to pray. Though I took you lightly, she never gave up. I went to church with her only on Christmas and Easter, but she loved and cared for me and continued secretly to pray for me and for her husband until late at night. Seeing Your continuous Light in my mother made me curious enough and encouraged continual fellowship. I became engrossed in the pastor's strong sermons. Though the pastor was just a man and the pulpit was made of wood, I could feel Your rich, warm love, peace, and joy.

I admired one of the families at the church. The father and mother sang in the choir and served on many committees. Their children were well behaved and sang in the junior choir. They were happy in spite of their poverty and gave thanks to You when their parents could afford to buy new shoes for them. I wasn't as thankful and happy as they were when I received my prized electric train for Christmas! Yes, Lord, You choose these and other precious people to reveal your brilliant light that I might one day emerge from my darkened world into Your sunshine of grace and bask in Your love.

What a wonder and a privilege that Your marvelous grace extends to me. For I am not one of Your Chosen people; I'm a gentile and a sinner, but You loved me so much that You suffered and died that I might become one of Your children! Lord, never allow me to take Your loving Grace for granted or have a haughty spirit. I am undeserving of your mercy; like a filthy drunken hobo who suddenly is given all the inheritance of a king! But praise be to You, Lord, Who made me an heir and called me Your Child. A child of the Living God, who formed all of creation, for I have come to believe in your Holy Name! I rejoice at being your child for only You in Your Superior Wisdom could send Your Son, Jesus, to cleanse me from all unrighteousness and make me pure, white as snow and adopt me into Your Royal Family!

JOHN 1:14-18

HUMBLE ME, LORD!

Good and gracious God, have mercy on me, and humble me, as You humbled Yourself to be born in a fleshly body and took the role of a servant for all of humanity. Let me, therefore, meditate on Your Greatness and behold Your Glory, for You're my Father, and are full of Grace and Truth! Teach me, Lord, never to set a limit on you or Your Greatness; never to put You on my level or standard of thinking, thus putting You in a tiny box. Just as I get tired and irritated at people who think they know who I am and what I can (or cannot)do - putting me in their tiny box! You also take offense at me whenever I try to limit You, thinking that you are capable of doing only certain things! I exalt You, for you are greater than I can imagine, far above other gods; Your Grace and truth are incomprehensible. I just accept You and what You are!

If anyone admires the qualities inside of me, let me point to You, Jesus, and say that you are the reason, and declare like John the Baptist that You are higher than I am. I give thanksgiving for pouring out Your Grace and Truth so freely and without measure for my salvation, justification, election, faith, and spiritual gifts. Through this grace and truth, I can do the impossible to see You, God – by Your Son, Jesus Christ, Who revealed Your glorious Light.

JOHN 1:19-28

NOT ME, BUT YOU, LORD!

People look far and wide for a leader they can follow, they long to trust, admire and then, subconsciously, that person becomes their God. Some admire me and the peace I have. They almost put me in the same category as an angel. I tell them the peace that I have is from You, Lord. That they can have the same qualities, by taking You, Christ, into their lives. They too shall have joy, love, and peace!

The day when You will come again isn't far off, allow me to dwell in You in order that my words and my life can reflect You and Your Love. May my words and my life be a message and a witness from You; that others would feel the need To make their hearts ready for You. But praise be to You, who makes me upright and righteous to show other sinners Your Way of life everlasting!

JOHN 1:29-34

THE PURE LAMB OF GOD

O Holy Lamb of God, thank You for Your Baptism that washes us clean with pure hearts, minds and eyes to see You. I repent and ask forgiveness for every one of my sins. I have need of You and Your Grace; I will humble myself under Your mighty reign! Thank you Jesus for coming and being so submissive to Your Father, to be baptized in the Holy Spirit so that Your spirit would dwell in me and bear witness to Your Most Holy Name. I give praise to You for letting me see You with Spirit Eyes. May my life become such a witness to Your Ways that everybody whom I contact will be driven to You and behold Your Glory.

JOHN 1:35-39

I'LL FOLLOW YOU, LORD

I follow You, Jesus, My Lord, like the disciples of old; though I often stumble and fall, I follow the path You lay before me. You accept and count me worthy to be Your Disciple, by seeking Your Will in my life, so You can lead and guide me. Lord I yield and give all my life to You; take complete control of me, my time, my talents, my money, my life. Steer me; You're my rudder. Mold me; I'm Your Clay! Cause me to remember that following You isn't easy; that nothing will go my way. Forgive me when I rebel, cry, and curse. When I have seen my sins, let me come running to your Loving Arms. You are my mighty teacher, Who supplies me with a lifetime of knowledge and wisdom. I remember the teachers who taught me well in school; they were tough but always smiled and were happy for me when they saw I was doing my best to learn. So I'll follow You Lord, though the road might get rocky. When times get tough, don't let me forget that my joy is in You! Yes, even though I have to spend the rest of my mortal life in this wheelchair, I will be glad in You and rejoice in my salvation; for if I had a strong body, the riches of a king, I would be poor, with no hope without You!

JOHN 1:40-42

PRAISE YOU FOR ACCEPTING ME

I praise You for accepting me for who I was and where I was when I first met You! You took me just as I was instead of expecting me to change my ways all at once. You just wanted me to love You; You molded me and continue to mold me in Your Image on my journey with You.

You called Peter to follow You, even though You knew that he would sometimes be of little faith and would deny you three times as his Lord. Likewise, You gave me the privilege of following You, in spite of Your foreknowledge that I was often to fail you. Yes, even before the foundations of the world, You knew that I was going to hurt and disappoint You, going against Your Will for my life, at times even by being ashamed to know You! But You remained faithful and believed in me in spite of all my failures. You lovingly corrected, and encouraged me to walk in paths of Your Righteousness. As You had patience with Peter, who spoke boldly of You, and became the leader of Your Church, so You are constantly perfecting me to become Your Servant, to be part of Your Body and to be a chip of Your Rock.

JOHN 1:43-51

PRAISE YOU FOR BRINGING GOOD OUT OF NOTHING

Oh, Nazareth!! What good and perfect gift came from your village that had been insignificant and of no reputation. The Messiah, for whom Israel waited centuries to deliver them, came from within your walls. Oh, Jesus, King of Israel, I praise You for coming from the tiny town of Nazareth. You didn't grow up living in a palace, but lived as other common men and worked with Your Hands as a carpenter. You didn't grow up as a prince or an earthly king; but You, in spite of being the Son of the Most-High

God, lived and dwelt among mankind so that You would know every heartache and disappointment. Praise be to You, for You not only experienced my every hurt, but You took away all the hurts by Your death on the cross.

You first saw me as You first saw Nathaniel sitting under the fig tree. I didn't know You, but You saw the hunger in my heart - devoid of a meaningful relationship with You. Though You created me with a soul to love and worship You, You waited patiently until I saw that I needed You and that I was lost without Your Grace. The night I first reached out to You was filled with such complete joy and wonder, impossible to duplicate; each day gets better and better as long as I am walking with You!

chapter two

Praise God for What He is

JOHN 2:1-5

PRAISE FOR A CLOSE RELATIONSHIP WITH JESUS

I give praise to You, Jesus; You're not only the King and God of this universe but my best Friend, and concerned about me wherever I go. You weren't ashamed or too dignified to attend the wedding at Cana, so also You aren't too proud to live inside of this fleshly, sinful body of mine; and to come with me to attend the social events of my day as long as I am walking in Your Will. Teach me to love and honor my parents and hold them in esteem as You respected Your Mother; You called her "woman" out of respect in those days.

As You respect me also, grant that I may respect and revere Your Holy Name. Teach me to fear Your Name and take You seriously as You commanded Your People not to even touch the mountain from which You talked to Moses lest You put them to death. Yes, help me to regard You seriously and to fear You with awe so that I might be obedient and seek Your Will. I will do whatever You say.

JOHN 2:6-11

PRAISE FOR THE LITTLE THINGS IN LIFE
(PERSONAL TESTIMONY)

Thank You, Lord, for the surprising little things that make my head shake in utter amazement and give me a greater appreciation and joy for my salvation and eternal life! Just as You had compassion turning water into wine so that all the guests could celebrate the wedding in Cana, You work miracles in my life, that causes chills up my spine and my hair to stand on end!

For so long my great desire was to have an electric-powered wheelchair with controls that I could operate with my head so that I could have the same freedom and mobility as some of my friends who could use their hands to drive their chairs. I received a powered chair, but with a mouth control that got in the way when I typed and painted, in addition to being very unsanitary. When I complained, my friends protested and fought for the head control that I wanted. You showed me and everyone around me that You were still God and had everything under control.

At an amusement park, I was hit by a tram. My inconvenient chair was badly damaged, but You protected me from getting one cut or scratch! You used the accident to bring good, as it was then possible for me to get the head control that I had wanted for so long. What I fought two years to achieve, You got for me in two weeks.

I was surprised again at Christmas time when You laid on the hearts of my friends to give me an expensive radio stereo when I would have settled for a transistor radio. I hear You saying: "I have given special things because You are My Child and are very special to me; and since you're My child and are walking in My ways, nothing is too good for you! "So ride in dignity and know that the blessings that You have received are from your God, because you are My child and Joint Heir with Me! Lord...Thank You for my overflowing cup for these and many other blessings - too many to count - as You filled the water pots to the brim with the water you turned to wine.

JOHN 2:12-17

PRAISE YOU FOR HATING SIN BUT LOVING SINNERS

O Holy God, I praise You for Your Purity, for there is no sin in Your midst; otherwise, You wouldn't be God. You look upon sin, or disobedience, as a plague that You'll have no part of, for it's not of You, Lord. Yes, Your Purity and Righteousness are white as snow; behold, a drop of ink in a clear glass of water makes the water cloudy and dirty, it's the same with man; one sin defiles him.

Just as you became angry as Your Temple was corrupted, so You get angry whenever I go against Your Will. Like my natural parents, who often got upset at the things I did as a child, but who never stopped loving me, so You, Lord, never stop loving me, even with Your foreknowledge of all my sins against You.

When others offend me by taking advantage or hurting me, may I be like You, Jesus, and get angry at their deeds — not at the individuals, for You love them as much as You love me; You bled and sacrificed Your Life for all. Help me love all my brothers and sisters the way You love them. Lamb of God, pure Lamb of God, thank You for insisting on having no sin in Your Midst so that I can be made righteous and pure through You! Holy, Holy, Holy God, thank You for Your pure standard.

JOHN 2:18-22

PRAISE YOU FOR SECURITY FORETOLD

Lord, may I look past the material blessings and meditate and rejoice at the victory of Your Resurrection from the dead and at my salvation in You! Just as You live and reign forever, so I will be resurrected with my new glorified body, unhindered; to dwell with You for eternity.

May I not be preoccupied with the successes and the events of the day, that my mind would not be trapped into limiting Your Great Power. The Jews couldn't figure out how You would destroy their temple and build another one in three days when it took them forty-six years to build the original one. Yes, all of man's resources of gold, silver, and other precious materials used to make the temple beautiful cannot match Your victorious resurrection so that I can sup with You and be in Your Presence! So, O Lord, let me meditate and rejoice in You, my temple, and may I abide in you forever!

JOHN 2:23-25

HELP ME TO KNOW YOU WITHOUT SEEKING
MIRACULOUS SIGNS
(PERSONAL TESTIMONY)

O Lord and my God, may I always accept You for who and what You are without relying on signs and wonders. The Joy, the Peace, and the Faith that You are with me is all that I need. To be in Your Presence is far better than to have my body healed or to leap out of my wheelchair in which I have been confined for 36 years! I ponder how tired you must get of men constantly seeking signs as if miracles alone could prove your Existence and Might. I become annoyed when people refuse to believe that I can do certain things like typing and painting in spite of my disabilities. I have to actually show them. So may I never challenge Your Sovereignty or Power; just to glory in Your Name should be more than sufficient. But realizing my doubting nature, You love me so much that You perform miracles every day of my life to assure me that You are there. Therefore, I give praise to You for understanding my human nature and loving me and accepting me with an unconditional love.

chapter three

Praise for God's Kingdom

JOHN 3:1-15

PRAISE FOR THE NEW LIFE IN YOU

I give praise for my new Life in You, Jesus, for opening my eyes to spiritual matters. Behold how much more to life there is than flesh and blood and the pleasures of this world! This earthly life lasts approximately 70 years; its pleasures hide all the gloom and sorrows that constantly have to be guarded so as not to be brought to the surface. But the life in You, Christ, transcends all the false, paradoxical niceties of this world and restores me back to fellowship with You to delight in giving glory, honor, and praise to Your Name! Yes, I am a new creature in You; The old things passed away; behold, all things have become new. Let me always be in awe and wonder at my new life!

JOHN 3:16-21

PRAISE FOR MY SALVATION

I give praise to You, Father, for the way of salvation in Your only begotten Son, Jesus Christ and that the only thing I am to do to make me acceptable to You is to believe that all my sins have been taken away. Your Way of Salvation requires only a child-like trust that even the simple minded or the physically impaired can act upon. I would be lost if receiving eternal life meant physically climbing a rock; knowing the Bible inside and out; or obtaining a certain status at church by doing so many good deeds. You offered Your Hand for me to reach out and hold, to be my advocate, and placed my sins on Your Shoulders.

Never allow me to think that Your son, Jesus, came to judge or condemn me, but rather to be a light in my once darkened world. At first, I hated the light as it revealed my sins which were done in darkness. Your Light exposed my sinful nature; it hurt like coming out of a pitch black tunnel into the light of a bright, sunny day. At first my eyes strained, but the longer they were exposed to the daylight the less my pupils hurt and the more I could behold the beauty and splendor of Your creation - the mountains, valleys, and seas. And the more I am exposed to You and Your Light the less it hurts to give up my evil ways and the more I delight in the Magnificent Glory of following Your righteous paths. So let my eyes always see Your Truth and Glory that all my ways may become Your ways, so that others may glorify You!

JOHN 3:22-30

PRAISE GOD I AM SOMEBODY BECAUSE HE IS SOMEBODY!!

I give all the praise to You, my Lord, for baptizing and purifying me. Thank You for humbling me and for restoring my life to a right fellowship with You. Yes, You are restoring me to Your image and to behold Your Glory so that I can be beautiful in Your sight. I hear Your voice quiet within me saying, "My child, My child, You are someone special to Me, because I am special in your life. Because you have made me your God, put Me first, and worshipped Me, I have made you My son and an heir of My kingdom. You know Me because I revealed Myself to You, and your spirit bore witness to the reality of my Spirit. You are my Bride and a member of My Holy Church; I am your bridegroom. Submit unto Me as a good wife submits to her husband who has her best interests at heart. The more you let Me increase in your life and humble yourself before Me, the more special you will become to Me and I will shower My blessings on you for everyone to see!" Praise, Honor, and glory to You, My God and King, You who are Holy and Righteous, You make me, Your son, acceptable in Your sight!

JOHN 3:31-36

PRAISE GOD FOR BEING A GENTLEMAN IN ALLOWING ME TO CHOOSE

Thank You, Lord, for loving me so much and being the gentleman that You are to allow my choice between matters of heaven or this world and to choose my own destiny. I saw what the world had to offer me; its pleasures lasted for only a little while, leaving me feeling empty and unfulfilled. I didn't know what I wanted. The things of this world do not satisfy me. But when I allowed You to come gently into my life, I wanted more of You and what You had to offer: Love, peace, and joy!

You didn't leave my heart empty and unsatisfied, You gave me and continue to give me Your bounteous riches. Thank You, Father, for giving Your Son, Jesus; Your Holy Spirit without measure and for giving Him all power, even the ultimate power and victory over sin. Oh, death, where is your victory and where is your sting; for all things, even death has been given to You, Jesus, and taken from the grips of Satan! Through You, Jesus, is the victory! I believe in You and offer thanksgiving for the gift of eternal life. Remind me of Your eternal wrath to those who are disobedient, though you are their Lord and Savior. Let me share with others Your gift of Eternal Life, for I have no monopoly on it.

chapter four

Praise God for His Compassion

JOHN 4:1-3

LORD TEACH ME NOT TO BE A PHARISEE

O Lord teach me not to be a Pharisee, by playing at religion and by placing limitations and restrictions on others, thus grieving Your Holy Spirit. You were unable to minister effectively to people in Judea and had to depart into Galilee to avoid the Pharisees who were endlessly debating and questioning You regarding your teachings. You may have felt the same way as I do, when some Christians become offended and rebuke me for partaking of Holy Communion with a dear friend, instead of being served by an ordained minister or a priest.

Lord, cause me to remember that "a woe and a judgment" is given to me if I tell a person to do one thing and I do the opposite! May Your Holy Spirit flow through me unhindered by anything I do. Instead may I be Your vessel ministering to others. Yes, may I always keep my eye on Your Mercies, so I can show forth Your merciful love to those whom I come in contact with on a daily basis, instead of passing judgment on them.

JOHN 4:4-26

BEING AN UNFORCEFUL FRIEND

Lord, Jesus, as You befriended the woman at the well, a Samaritan, a social outcast in Your day, so may I be an unforceful friend to others who are down-trodden, aged, and perhaps those who would embarrass me. Let me be sensitive enough to discern the occasions when you would have me witness Your Grace and Saving Power by establishing friendships with another thirsty soul. Who likes to be preached at when they are hurting? And who wants to listen, when they have needs to be met or when they crave a listening ear! Have me always listen and respond to needs of people; for if my love is genuine and real, their curiosity will lead them to Your Living Water inside of me. Just as a fawn senses there's a stream to drink from over the next hill, so may the friends that I make become thirsty for an unknown quality seen in me.

That unknown quality is You, Jesus! May You over flow through my soul with Your sweet Holy Spirit and Living Waters. As my friends first drink of Your Living Water, never let me be quick to condemn them for their sins, for the more they fall in love with You and experience a right relationship with You, the more they want to repent and change their ways to please You. For You are the only True God, who is worthy to be praised by all men and nations because our joy and salvation is found in You! Yes, You alone are worthy to be praised by all men! You even adopted me a non-Jew, a Gentile into Your family,

JOHN 4:27-38

PRAISE FOR YOUR SPIRITUAL FOOD

Lord, never let me be gluttonous and hog all Your Spiritual Food for myself and my friends. There are plenty of hungry souls in the world. Your Plan of Salvation through Jesus Christ isn't for a group or clique but for the world. Lord, forgive me for being, as Your Disciples were, outdone by the woman at the well and by new believers who enthusiastically tell everyone about You. Freshen my love for You that my enthusiasm to tell everyone about You will be that of new believers, for indeed my food isn't of this world, but to do your Will, Father God, to share the abundant life which only You can give! Make me more sensitive to hungry souls in need of Your Spiritual Food and of Your great love! Teach me to reap and to sow, and give me discernment when to do each; for in so doing I do Your Will, laying up for me treasures in heaven and gathering fruit for Eternal Life.

JOHN 4:39-42
PRAISE FOR INDEPENDENT FAITH IN YOU

Continue to make me a follower of Yours only, Jesus, and let my faith not be dependent on other believers, but by the special relationship between us. Before I took Your Hand and had a firm foundation in Your Word, I admired some friends and relatives who believed in You because I saw Your Shining Light in them. But the moment I chose to make You the personal Lord and Saviour of my life I began to fall in love with You and to have a unique relationship with You. People may say they see and hear You and believe in Your Name, but only when I believed on my own did the purpose and fulfillment of my life begin to be revealed.

So, Lord, I give You Holy Praise that the purpose and fulfillment of my life is to know and believe that You love me and to fall deeper and deeper in love with You from now until eternity!

Praise You, God, for loving me and thank You for allowing me to love You in return, thus making a very special relationship between us!

JOHN 4:43-45

PRAISE YOU FOR BEING VULNERABLE

I praise You, Jesus, for returning to Galilee, though You had the foreknowledge that You would be hurt and rejected and had no honor among Your countrymen. How lonely You must have felt and how hurt You must have been to go into Your country where people didn't believe in You. Even Your brother, James, didn't believe in whom You claimed to be. It would be as if I would move back to my old neighborhood and attend the old traditional church in which I grew up. At first they would welcome me and would be glad to see me again, but after seeing my love and enthusiasm for You they might think I am a religious fanatic for talking about you and the Pastor's sermon after the church service instead of talking about who's going to win the pennant or who did what the past week, or even how to meet the church budget.

I hope that my old church would have enough love for You that this wouldn't happen, but if it did my heart would feel very sad indeed; not that I am any better than they, but they'd be missing out on the greatest blessing in having a love affair with You! I would feel very sad and hurt. You felt the rejection much more, rejecting You, God incarnate, by Your countrymen who expected the Messiah! Yet, You entered Your country. You could have performed Your ministry in an ivory palace far removed from anyone who would hurt You, but Your Love far out weighed all rejections or hurts encountered! Praise and honor to You, Lord that You loved the whole world even though You knew that it would have a great cost in heartache and finally death!

JOHN 4:46-52

PRAISE FROM THE OFFICIAL OF CAPERNAUM
(FROM HIS VIEW POINT)

Praise You, Jesus, for bringing me back to the days when You lived on earth, and for letting me imagine myself to be the Capernaum official, whose son was healed from the point of death. I hear his testimony saying:

"I didn't know what to do, for my child was in bed dying; my wife and I tried everything the best physicians and the latest medicine but he didn't seem to get any better. One day I heard that a man named Jesus had returned to Cana of Galilee, (where the king had stationed me). I remembered that this same Jesus turned water into wine. So I thought I'd ask Him to use His magical powers to heal my son. What did I have to lose! When I asked Him to perform a miracle to restore my son's health, I saw hurt in His eyes as he said, 'Unless you people see signs and wonders You simply will not believe!' Then I sensed that He was more than a great magician, and I pleaded with Him to come with me and heal my son. He must have seen my faith in Him and told me to go home, for my child had been healed!"

"I knew He was sincere, so I started to Capernaum to see how my son was. I was concerned still, but inside of me was a joyous expectation that a miracle had taken place in my child's condition. On the way one of my servants came running to meet me with good news; sure enough, my little son had been healed! I saw for myself that my child was fine, even jumping and playing. I asked when he began to get better. I found out that it was the same hour that Jesus said that he lived!"

"Not only did Jesus make my son to live but He later died on the cross so that my boy would never die but live forever with Him! And this same Jesus, not only made the boy to live forever, He saved me and my entire family, as well as the rest of humanity who has believed in His Holy Name, from the gates of hell to the glory and splendor of Heaven! Glory, honor, and praise belongs to Jesus, who gives us all victory to live forevermore in the Presence of His Father and to claim the liberty! Amen! Praise the Lord!"

chapter five

Praise God for His Power

JOHN 5:1-9

PRAISE FOR GIVING POWER TO THE POWERLESS
(PERSONAL EXPERIENCES)

Lord, my heart is awe struck and rejoices at the miracle healing of the man, disabled for 38 years; I know how it is to be
physically and mentally impaired for such a long time. How helpless I feel when I want to get out of bed and can't without help.
If I were to attempt it myself, I would land on the floor as I have
done before. I remember the struggle a friend had. He slipped
and fell in a room alone with me. Although he could walk with
braces and crutches, his legs were completely paralyzed from
polio; he had to get off the floor by himself. I couldn't go for
help. I didn't have an electric wheelchair. I was as helpless as he
was. He could usually get up from the ground by pushing his
body up with his arms like push-ups, but the floor was too slip-
pery and he couldn't get any traction. His paralyzed legs would
go as they pleased, as if from a rag doll. He tried again and again

to get up. The bottom half of his body wouldn't cooperate, always finding a leg or two in the most unlikely positions. Finally, he used his arms to drag his body to where I was sitting so that he could use my chair to pull himself up. The man, at Bethesda, disabled for 38 years, must have felt similar struggles as he tried the best he could with whatever was functioning to inch himself in the water and be healed, only to find that another made it in to the water before him. You, Jesus, saw this man's struggle, being in such a helpless condition for years, and asked him if he would like to be healed. You were so patient as you listened to him pour out his inner feelings, explaining the impossibility of getting into the water so that the angel could heal him. But You had compassion for him and ignored his human mind. You spoke the Word, which commanded all authority; he was made whole, with no effort on his part and without an angel.

I love You, Lord; Your Power overwhelms me. You not only mended his spinal cord or whatever was debilitating him, but You straightened his bones and all of his muscles, inactive for years, so that he could use his legs instantly and carry his pallet. What a tremendous sight it would be if you chose to instantly heal me, Lord Jesus. You first would repair my brain cells, damaged at birth. You would straighten out parts of my body twisted from sitting a certain way in my wheelchair all my life. Then You would give strength to muscles I haven't used for 36 years. Maybe You would make me 40 or 60 pounds heavier, for my developed body weighs only 88 pounds! Praise You, Lord, for Your Mighty Power; for You not only heal and mend at the very core of a problem even the brightest scientists and doctors can't solve, You also take care and work everything out to the finest detail.

JOHN 5:9-18

PRAISE FOR NOT GOING BY THE BOOK

I praise You, Lord Jesus, for the freedom and liberty You possess, for I am not bound or condemned by rules and regulations men think are Yours. How sad that the people criticized the man who was healed for carrying his pallet. You told him You were more interested in the purity of his heart towards You than by being bogged down by the strict laws of the Sabbath. Isn't that why You told him not to sin anymore, to be in Your Will and seek Your Righteousness. You saw him in the Temple rejoicing and expressing thanksgiving to you for the miracle in his life.

Lord Jesus, I need Your forgiveness when I criticize some of my brothers and sisters in the body and think that they should be more spiritual and not be ashamed to openly sing praises and lift their hands to You. For You are at work in each person who You made differently and magnificently with thought processes, traits, and personalities all of their own! If I see an old lady quietly kneeling on a pew bench in a traditional church, it would remind me that it was the Virgin Mary who pondered the birth of Jesus, Saviour of the world, in her heart. Lord, never allow me to impose my own rules and regulations on others, but make me more sensitive to begin to see the sincerity of hearts the way that you do.

JOHN 5:19-29

PRAISE FOR PERFECT UNITY

Thank You, Father God and Lord Jesus, for working together in perfect unity to accomplish Your Will on earth and in my life. How refreshing it is that You have no power struggles (Father, Son & Holy Ghost). Teach me the same quality and mold me in Your Image, so that nothing else matters except to be in Your Will and to love You! You made everything in the Universe beautifully and I stand in awe of it. You sent Your Son to lead me in the sunshine of Your Grace that I might marvel now and forever more. Lord, Jesus, I honor You as my Saviour; I honor You, my Heavenly Father, as Creator; Yes, I give you honor, glory, and praise as you redeemed me to be acceptable in the sight of the Father. You, Jesus, by Your death on the cross and by the power of Your Resurrection made it possible for me to live in eternity also, as well as to dwell on earth in the Spirit of Father God.

Let me so abide in You that I won't be surprised when I see You open all the graves and tombs of those who have lived before, to give new life and new bodies to decaying skeletons and bones, most of which have turned to dust and ashes. What an awesome thought and what a magnificent sight this will be! I will have eternal life instead of being judged, simply because I believed in Your wonderful Grace!

JOHN 5:30-47

PRAISE FOR GIVING WITNESSES TO YOU

Thank You, Jesus, for being in the perfect will of God, Your Father and mine; You are just and wise. How blessed it is to know that those who lie, cheat, and act wickedly against me will be given their just reward by what You and the Father deem best! Never allow me to take vengeance on those who do me wrong, for Your punishment is much more severe and sometimes more swift than I could mete. Even in my life on planet earth I see You administering justice. I remember when a comrade was harassing me, I prayed for You to take care of the situation. She fell and broke her leg! Ah, I felt so special to be Your child. You protected and delivered me from her evil ways!

What a great God You are, and how just are Your Ways. Thank You for revealing to me, through the witness of the Father, that You are the only true Messiah and the only Saviour of mankind. For You understand my logical mind, and created my reasoning process in such a way that You know that I need the virility of the Father to bear witness to You, the Son of God! You not only had Your Father to give witness that Your are true, but the multitude of fulfilling prophecies and the Holy Bible, as well as the miracles I have seen and have heard of, pointing to Your credibility to be my Saviour! Yes, indeed, You are the Son of God and my personal Saviour. You aren't like Buddha or other false messiahs who long since died; their bodies still buried in the ground. But You rose from the dead and are still living even today, to intercede with Your Father to forgive all sins on my behalf!

Thank You, Heavenly Father, for revealing Your Glory through Your Son, Jesus Christ, who goes between You, Most High God, and myself to take both of our hands and join us together. Thank You so much, Jesus, that I finally saw You as my Saviour through the witness of the Father, whose Spirit is within me, unlike the Jewish people who sought glory from themselves! No, I am no greater than they are; but I am sanctified and washed by Your Blood. I am saved from eternal damnation because You have shown me, through Your Glory, that you are my one and only Saviour! Glory, honor, and praise belong to You forever for showing me the power and the gift of Your Salvation!

AMEN!

chapter six

Praise God for His Abundance

JOHN 6:1-14

PRAISE GOD FOR MAKING SOMETHING OUT OF NOTHING

O Lord, how magnificent You are, abounding in mercy, for You knew that over 5,000 people were hungry when You multiplied five barley loaves to fill and satisfy the multitude! My response to Your question, Jesus, "where are we to buy bread so the 5,000 can eat"? would have probably been the same as Phillips's; panicking and stating the over-whelming impossibility in accomplishing such a feat. But You are the God of the impossible, and there is nothing too difficult for You. After all, You and the Father created the earth and the entire universe without a single atom at your disposal! You were the one who made the first atom! Is it any wonder that it was such an insignificant thing for You to feed the 5,000 and to do the many miracles in my Life?

O Lord, my Lord, how great and magnificent You are, not only to provide me with all that I need but to be my blessed Redeemer and Messiah, Who was prophesied of, even in the days of Moses!

JOHN 6:15

PRAISE YOU, JESUS, FOR NOT BECOMING AN EARTHLY KING

Praise and thanksgiving to You, Lord Jesus, for not being persuaded to become a king to those who wanted You as their political leader to solve the problems of the Roman Empire. If You were to have accepted the kingship of the Jewish people, You would not only have excluded the Romans from Your Love and Grace, but the whole Gentile world for 2,000 years - including me; I would have no hope!

Teach me to become like You, Lord; to go off alone to commune and have fellowship with the Father when life's circumstances seem to dictate what I should do. I want You to tell me what to do, even at risking unpopularity. Oh, how I love all Your Ways!

JOHN 6:16-21

PRAISE YOU, JESUS, FOR BEING LORD OVER NATURE

Praise You for being above the laws of nature, for being unbounded by the laws; after all, You made them and You can break natural laws any time You want! You were the Light that shined alone when You walked on the stormy sea to meet Your disciples late one night. No one had done this before. Yes, this supernatural feat was something to behold, and yet so natural for You, being the God You are! And at a moment's notice, when Your Disciples received You into their boat, You cleared up the storm and calmed the sea. Likewise, teach me to totally trust and receive You as Lord in days of trouble; to either calm the storm or ride with You on the waves. Yes, Lord, teach me to trust You in good days, as well as bad.

JOHN 6:22-40

MATERIAL VS. SPIRITUAL (PERSONAL EXPERIENCE)

Thank You, Lord, for giving me the Bread of Life that I will never be hungry and Living Water so that I will never be Spiritually thirsty either and for giving the gift of eternal life! When You lived on earth the people sought you for the visual signs and wonders instead of the biggest miracle: Your Gift of Eternal Life, as well as, love, peace, and joy! How they missed out on what You had to offer them! How I missed out before I came to know You, Jesus! My greatest thing in life was dad's 1957 Ford Country Squire. It was in a car show before he bought it. What a great looking car it was, with its baby-blue color and wood-grain paneling! I loved its chrome-plated tail pipes that rumbled with the sound of the powerful V-8 engine. Soon the beautiful station wagon became old as the fake wood paneling faded from the heat of the sun and the chrome-plated tail pipes had to be replaced by regular black pipes. I become fond of other cars that were newer, only to discover that they eventually fall apart and become old. My dad traded the once fancy Country Squire for a plain ordinary station wagon that was newer; I was constantly searching for things to satisfy me, but nothing would for very long.

But when I met You, Jesus, all my desires and longings were satisfied; and after knowing you for these past 18 years, You have never become old, like my seemingly precious processions did. Yes, You give me Bread of Life, and give me Living Water to fill the hunger and thirst within my soul; You are my Lord, in whom I have everything I could ever ask for!

JOHN 6:41-65

PRAISE GOD FOR JESUS, THE LIVING BREAD

O my soul, do not be bound by old traditions. The Jews of old and the disciples expected the Bread of Life to be the manna in the wilderness. Let me open up instead to You, Jesus, the Bread of Life, and receive the gift of Eternal Life, to be grounded and rooted in You, to obtain all of Your Richest Blessings. Let my soul meditate on the awesome glory of Eternal Life where I shall live with You forever! Behold, Eternal Life has no end! Its presence of Love, Peace, and Joy lasts forever, as endless as looking into the starry heavens! Lord, Jesus, let me eat the Bread of Your Flesh and drink the Wine of Your Blood that I may be fully Yours! I believe in You completely. I come to You by faith, in spite of my unanswered questions; setting my eyes on only the Father, who reveals the truth, Jesus!

JOHN 6:66-71

PRAISE GOD FOR KNOWING MY HEART BETTER THAN I

O Lord, my God, let my soul be on guard lest my heart become haughty and refuse any longer to walk with You. Many of Your Disciples withdrew from You as they didn't comprehend what You were trying to teach them. They followed You because of the miracles they saw. Lord, I don't want to base my belief on mountain-top experiences, then fall away from You when I don't hear or understand You. Teach me not to be cocky about my personal relationship with You. Even Peter, as bold as he was, denied You three times; Judas Iscariot, one of Your twelve disciples betrayed You. Yet when I refuse to walk with You or seem to betray you at times, You never flee from me. Your Love is always near, ready to minister to me when I come back. Such love, oh my God! I truly cannot comprehend, but I praise and worship You for the abundant love in You!

chapter seven

Praise God for Choosing His Kingdom

JOHN 7:1-13

PRAISE YOU FOR LOVING THE WORLD WHO HATES YOU

My soul blesses You, Jesus, for disregarding what I first thought of You; not taking You seriously as the only True and Living God, as my Lord and Savior. How sad You must have felt when Your own half brothers made cynical remarks, not believing You were the Messiah! But You knew before-hand that they would reject You. Yes, You accepted the fact that the world hated and still hates You! How awesome is the thought that the people in the world, Your wonderful Creation, hate you!

You in Your Great Love are willing to give everyone a second chance to believe and come to Your Grace. You not only forgave Your brothers, who later came to believe in You, but You came with Your out-stretched arms to embrace me when I confessed You as my God! I praise You for being the personal God that You are! You forgave me the same way as You forgave Your own brothers and You love me the same way as You loved them!

JOHN 7:14-24

PRAISE YOU FOR KNOWING YOUR AUTHORITY

Teach me, Lord Jesus, to be more like You, to make sure my thoughts and ideas are as Your Father desires. Just as You did the works that the Father said to do, may I know and listen to You, that I can obey You and do whatever You say. For You, Father, who created the world, know everything thousands of years before an event happens. I want my will to be lined up with Yours. Yes, no amount of education, not even a Ph.D., can match up the knowledge You give me. My thoughts and ideas, apart from You, are puffed up in conceit, but whenever I do Your will in my life, I give glory and honor to You.

Let me do Your Will, Lord, no matter how others may criticize me, just as the Jews criticized You for healing a man on the Sabbath. Thank You for encouraging those who criticized You to seek the will of the Father before passing judgment.

JOHN 7:25-29

PRAISE YOU FOR KNOWING FROM WHERE YOU CAME

I give thanks and praise to You, Lord Jesus, in this age of insecurity with everyone asking themselves from where they came, that You know You were born of Your Father, who You helped form the world. Never allow me to wonder and philosophize Your origin, for Your Word says that Your Father sent You and I am secure in You. I know that I am Your Child! Thank You for such security and for a sure foundation in You; because of You I not only know from where I came but know to where I am going!

JOHN 7:30-36

WHAT CAN WE DO WITH THIS JESUS!
(FORMER PHARISEE'S VIEWPOINT)

We, the Pharisees, who nit-pick anyone disobeying the Law, didn't know what to do about this Jesus, who broke all of our traditions - healing people on the Sabbath day. Many people believed in Him and believed that he would do many more miracles, so we tried to arrest Him before the crowd got too carried away. Just before we were to seize Him, we heard Jesus tell the people that the time hadn't come for Him to be arrested. He was saying that the place to which He was going was the place that the persons sent Him. And none of them could go with Him. Little did we know that He was going to Heaven to prepare a place for me; I had thought He was going to be a missionary to the Greeks and the Gentiles, who we, the Pharisees, despised.

I later followed the rest of the Pharisees to help arrest and crucify Him, even though I sensed something genuine and sincere about this Jesus. After he rose from the dead, being sure that He was indeed the Son of God, I received forgiveness of my sins which He graciously offered to me and to the rest of mankind. It's hard to believe, but although I harmed Him physically, I am redeemed and sanctified along with you, the reader. Join with me, a former hypocritical Pharisee, in giving Jesus all the glory and praises He deserves for giving us another chance to be with God, now and through eternity!

JOHN 7:37-39

PRAISE YOU FOR QUENCHING MY THIRST FOREVER-MORE

I give all thanks and praise to You, Jesus, forevermore quenching my thirst from the Rivers of Living Water, that gives me Your precious Holy Spirit. As a drink of ice tea on a hot summer's day relieves my parched lips and dry throat, so my soul welcomes Your Spirit to strengthen and comfort me and to freshen my day. Thank You, Lord, that I need not wait until Pentecost, as your disciples did, for your blessed Holy Spirit to fall but that the living Water is always ready to tap for as long as I want and in any amount. Lord, don't let me turn off the faucet, let me drench myself in Your Spirit!

JOHN 7:40-53

PRAISE GOD FOR SIMPLE PEOPLE

Thank You, Lord, for creating me simply so that I can believe that You are the Christ - The Messiah, and not merely a prophet or some religious fanatic. People who are highly educated, as the Pharisees, who argue theology, question who You are and from where You came. Thank You for Your Grace (there was no Grace under the Law), that doesn't condemn. If I am disobedient, thank You, Lord, for having mercy upon me!

chapter eight

Praise Be To Jesus for His Righteous Judgement

JOHN 8:1-11

A FRIEND COMES TO BAT FOR ME

I love You, Jesus, for coming to bat for me while my friends and others condemn and persecute me for the wrongs and sins I may have committed. How embarrassed the woman must have felt when the scribes and the Pharisees brought her as You were teaching many in the temple. They had caught her in the very act of adultery! What shame she must have felt not only for the adulterous sin she had committed but for being made a spectacle of before the crowd. You tried to continue teaching, ignoring the scribe's and the Pharisee's accusations. You knew they were trying to trap You into an opinion. But they kept pressing You to address the subject instead of dealing with it privately. How gracious are You, Lord, when they persisted, You said if anyone hadn't any sin in his life he should cast the first stone, to stone her to death for her immoral act. Nobody could say he was without sin, so they left You and the woman alone, and You dealt with her personally, and simply told her not to sin anymore.

Lord, let my mind wander to a point in my life, even back to my childhood, where I might have sinned and I was made a public spectacle for what I did wrong. I will remember when I was extremely embarrassed by one of my parents, a teacher or a friend who scolded me in front of my friends or a group for something I did wrong. In the midst of feeling embarrassed, wishing that I could dig a hole to hide myself, I now see You Jesus, entering the picture, as Your Very Presence and Righteous Judgment silence my mockers. You walk closer to me and all others faint away; I say, "I'm sorry and I won't do it again." You don't look angry but full of compassion for me. You get even closer to me, and Your face is the only thing I see; You look into my heart and You see the hurt from the mockers (that I have hidden a long time ago). Then You seem to say, "I know you're sorry; I forgave you long ago when you asked me to. I come now to take away the hurt and embarrassment. Give to me the hurt and forgive those who shamed you! I am making you clean, just as I forgave the woman for committing adultery and cleansed her from her guilt."

JOHN 8:12-20

PRAISE YOU, JESUS, FOR YOUR LIGHT FROM THE FATHER

All hail and adoration to You, Jesus, Who gives light to live life; You show me Your Father's light and it illuminates my path. Like a flashlight that lights my way so that I won't stumble into a hole on a pitch-dark night, so You light up my path that I might not fall into sin and so that I can see Your Father and His Will for my life. Let me see Your Light, Jesus, that I might see Your Father; His Truth and Righteous Judgment and His Splendid Majesty, for You and the Father are one.

JOHN 8:21-47

PRAISE YOU, FOR BEING GOD,YET MY REDEEMER

I bless You, my Jesus, for hiding my sins in their ugliness from Your Father and for forgiving my sins simply because I believe that You are the Son of God. Like the Jews in Your time on earth, I hate when my sins are exposed, and I try to deny any wrong, wishing that I could dig a hole for myself to hide in. Not saying that You told me so, You showed me that I am from below - of the world, living in sin - and that You are from above, living in full Glory of God, the Father. Yet You so willingly bridge the gap and reach Your loving arms to me when I humble myself enough and believe, You come right back from Your Glory to take away my sins and to set me free with the truth of the knowledge of Who You are! Thank You, my God, that I am not a slave to sin, rejecting the truth that You freely give - never let it be!

JOHN 8:48-58

PRAISE YOU, JESUS, FOR LIVING AN AGELESS LIFE

Praise and glory to You, Jesus, for being so patient and understanding when I don't understand Your Godly attributes and when I try to fit You into my human concepts. Help me to not deny Your Glory given by the Father God, or the blessings of Eternal Life that You give me, as You gave the people on earth. Help me not to be bound by my own concept of twentieth century time, for you lived before Abraham and Adam and even before time began. You are the GREAT I AM and there is unmatched power in Your name, the Eternal Existent One.

JOHN 8:58

PRAISE YOU, JESUS, FOR MIRACULOUSLY AVOIDING THE STONING

Lord of Lords and King of Kings, the people wanted to stone You to death as punishment for blasphemy for claiming to be the Eternal God. Surely the jagged rocks and stones would have bruised, cut, and hurt your incarnate, human body as the stones pounded and hit you, like the forceful rain as it splatters the streets. Remind me that You had a body like mine. You experienced pain like I do. Life is not the Hollywood-movie image of being hurt one moment and okay the next. It was a miracle that You came out alive. You performed this miracle because You had work to do, including saving me from my sins! Praise You forever, Lord Jesus!

chapter nine

Praise TO Jesus, THE Light Of THE World

JOHN 9:1-5

PRAISE YOU FOR MANIFESTING YOUR GLORY
(PERSONAL INSIGHTS)

Oh my dear and precious Lord, thank you for doing a marvelous work with the man who was born blind who later could see physically, as well as, spiritually. You first dealt with the issue of the blindness resulting from his or his parents' sin. My parents and I have also been confronted by critics. In this circumstance, You said that sin wasn't the cause of the man being blind - thus freeing him from condemnation - but that Your Power and Glory would be revealed, through his condition. For the first time in all of history, through the works of Your Father, the blind man was healed, enabling him to see as never before!

Lord, help me not to gloss over this miracle lest I suddenly and unexpectedly go blind for the rest of my life. You are the God of the impossible; You gave sight to the blind man who had been in total darkness all of his life. Thank You for the miracles You did while You were on earth. You have the same miracle-working power today. You can and will heal me of my affliction with Cerebral Palsy at Your appointed time, just as you waited to heal the blind man at Your own pre-selected time! You and You alone can accomplish this, You made our bodies, You are familiar with every cell, muscle, and joint. You are the Light of the World to make the blind see and make me walk!

JOHN 9:6-12

PRAISE YOU FOR MEETING ME WHERE MY FAITH IS.

Lord, I praise You for Your restorative healing Powers, for Your Grace and Loving-kindness and for meeting me at my level of faith. For surely You could have asked Your Father, who spoke Heaven into existence, to bring sight to the beggar. But You choose to meet him at his level of faith by making clay for his eyes and telling him to wash them at the pool of Siloam. What a captivating event it must have been for the blind man to see for the first time, encompassing the beauty of the surrounding hills that enclosed the desert filled with wild flowers and seeing every shade of blue, green, yellow, red, orange, brown, black and white! But all the colors in the rainbow and all the beauty in earth and heaven couldn't remotely compare with excitement and wonder of seeing Your Majestic Face, Jesus, The Son of the Living God who the blind man was about to know in an intimate way; behold, the beauty of Your Smile! Why, oh why, Lord, did some of his neighbors refuse to believe in Your Healing Powers? Why did they think the once blind man was an imposter? Yet, You in Your great Love accepted and loved them in their doubting that You do miracles as You still love and don't give up on me whenever I haven't enough faith in You.

JOHN 9:13-23

PRAISE YOU LORD FOR THE FREEDOM TO BELIEVE IN YOU

I give praise and adoration to You, Lord, for giving me the freedom to believe in You and Your miracle-working Power! One day You healed a blind man. His parents were afraid to tell the Pharisees Who had healed their son; they lived in constant fear much like those who are afraid to confess You because they live in communist countries. I thank You that my church believes in Your Power. Some churches might excommunicate me for believing that You can heal today, like the parents who were afraid of their son being thrown out of the synagogue for confessing You as the Christ, Messiah. I praise Your Holy Name for my country and church and that I am free to love and worship You! Cause me to remember in prayer those in other countries who aren't as fortunate, and are killed or sentenced to prison just for reading the Bible. Instill in me a sense of privilege and the priceless possession of Your Word that I hold in my hand, so that I can get to know the Mind and Heart of My Lord and My God!

JOHN 9:24-34

PRAISE FOR YOUR PERSISTENCE (FROM THE BLIND MAN'S VIEWPOINT)

I praise You, Father, for the persistence in the man who was healed of blindness. I can sense the frustration of this man when his friends and neighbors refused to believe that he was the one born blind and who begged for a living. I can hear him say: "I don't know anything about the man who healed me. But surely I know this; I was blind all my life. I couldn't see an inch in front of me, and now, by this unexplainable miraculous way, I see! Why do all of you want me to tell you this again and again? I am not lying, and why in heaven's name would I lie? Yet you revile me and say that I am dishonoring my Jewish religion all because I have told you that this man, whom you call Jesus, healed my eyesight. How do you account for this amazing thing; I was once totally blind, but by some power of His I can see for the first time in my life? Surely this man must be of God. Our God doesn't listen to the prayers of the unjust but to those who do His Holy Will and who hold Him in awesome respect. For the first time in human history, a man born blind, sees, for Jesus healed me!"

I praise You, Lord, for the fine witness of You that gave him such a determined heart to believe in You, and reverence before he knew who You really were. I thank You for putting the same kind of reverent respect in my heart and spirit to respect and fear the things of God before I saw You as my Lord and Master.

JOHN 9:35-41

PRAISE GOD FOR GIVING ME SPIRITUAL INSIGHTS

What a fantastic thing it must have been for the blind man to see for the first time, something even more beautiful than the most spectacular sunset, or mountain; that is seeing You as the Son of Man, and Your Great Love for me! All praise and honor I offer up unto You, for bringing me to a saving knowledge of what You did on the cross. Thank You for uncovering my eyes that I could see how beautiful You are; You alone and Your Marvelous Grace are all I see. Seeing You revealed my sins, but seeing into You took all my sins away. How sad it is for those who think they see You and have got it all together and they are good people and are church goers! Those who truly see You are those who know they have nothing to offer, that their lives could never be pleasing to You, but they desperately need You to take them out of their pit of miry clay. Lord, keep me humble and cause me to love You like the drug addict who recently came to You with the countenance of an expectant mother; he has the glow and sparkle in his eyes which shows a love affair with You.

chapter ten

Praise FOR THE Loving Shepherd

JOHN 10:1-18

PRAISE THE SHEPHERD FOR CARING FOR HIS FLOCK

Jesus, my true and loving Shepherd, I give praise and thanksgiving to You for being a safe-guard and guide in my spiritual walk with You. I am as a dumb sheep; before I learned to follow You, I followed the ways of the world and listened to every voice but Yours. But I heard You at the door calling my name so tenderly and assuredly to come into Your Pastures. Oh, how I love You and Your Presence; it's heaven to me! I'll never know why You called me to fellowship with You, God of the Most High. I often wander from Your Presence and Green Pastures; I forget to pray and seek hard after Your will. I take the road that is pleasing to me, but later I find that the road that looked so good to me is nothing but trouble, leading to death, destruction and hell. But before I go too far, I hear Your still and quiet voice again, and I am reminded of the abundant blessings in living for You and

Your Father. Jesus, You are my good and loving shepherd; nothing else I want, for Your Loving-kindness abounds to me; it is everlasting.

My good Shepherd, I praise You, for I know that You really care for me, unlike my attendants. Yes, these attendants may satisfy my needs temporarily, but when the going gets a little tough they take off as though they never knew me. But You are not that kind of God; not only do you stick with me through thick and thin, but You willingly laid down Your Life for me by hanging and dying on the cross so that Your Father would not see the evil things in my life. Praise You! You didn't lay down Your Life just for me, but You were resurrected as the Good Shepherd for as many in this wide world as receive You!

JOHN 10:19-21

PRAISE GOD FOR LETTING ME DECIDE

I thank and praise You, Lord, for allowing me to decide who You are even if it means insulting Your Divine Character; some thought that You were a demon, a madman. For all that they knew, You could have consumed them with fire at the snap of Your finger, for calling the very God who made this universe a demon and a mad man. But You loved them and love me. You have grace and mercy on me for the times past when I insulted Your Godly Character by thinking and saying that You are less than You are; Lord, forgive me! Lord, I not only thank You for the people who believed in You in Your day but for the people who influenced me to dedicate my life to You.

JOHN 10:22-30

PRAISE GOD FOR YOUR LOVING VOICE

My dear and beautiful Lord, I praise You for Your tender and loving Voice, which calls out my name and calls me to Your fold. May I hear Your Voice all the days of my life and may I follow Your Way, living in security of Eternal Life. Oh, how I love to hear the promise that I will never perish and that no one will be able to snatch me from Your Father! But woe to those who do not hear Your Voice, who are snatched up by other gods. I commit them in prayer, for they perish in everlasting fire. Father, I know that You are far greater than billions of people, in times past, in times present, and in the future, who have followed You. All praise I give You Jesus, for being one with Your Father and for both of You being concerned about my best interests as one of Your sheep.

JOHN 10:31-39

LET ME BE A LOVER OF YOUR WORKS

Instead of hating You, Jesus, for claiming to be God, instead of taking Your miracles for granted before You became Lord of my life, let me be a lover of Your works. I give all praise to You for Your works - both small and great - from the cool breeze in the summertime to the salvation that I have in You. I see Your Mighty Works in providing the best of Your people to care for all my needs and in giving me a place where I can meditate upon You in the peace and quiet of my home. Lord, I believe by these and other works that occur every second of the day that You are the Son of the Living God!

JOHN 10:40-42

PRAISE GOD WHO NEVER DISAPPOINTS

How I love and cling to a man of good reputation; a man whom I can count on as John counted on You, Jesus. All praise and thanksgiving to You Who never disappoints. The best of friends and family members can disappoint but You are my God and friend forever, faithful, you never let me down. Let many more believe in You and trust Your faithfulness, secure that You are the only one in Whom they can truly put their trust.

chapter eleven

Praise for Making the Dead Live

JOHN 11:1-16

PRAISE JESUS FOR BRINGING GLORY TO THE FATHER.

Lord of Lords and King of Kings, let me marvel at how You bring glory out of the most tragic circumstances, even sickness and death of Lazarus. You take the worst attack of the devil and turn it around with such great ease, to bring glory to Your Holy Name and the Father's. Satan is no match for You, Jesus, no matter how he tries to get me down You come and lift me up by turning the situation around for good. Remind me, Lord, that You are still in control of every situation regardless of how far away You may appear. I praise You for the fact that You are here at the times when I feel that you are a million miles away; even then, You don't condemn me for feeling this way; praise You, Jesus!

Lord remind me to take the message of Your Salvation while it is still day to the lost and dying world, as You did when it was still light out, instead of waiting for the hopeless and dangerous night.

JOHN 11:17-29

PRAISE JESUS FOR BEING THE RESURRECTION AND THE LIFE

Jesus, I love and adore You and I marvel at Your Greatness; You give me much more than I ask for. You gave more than Martha and Mary hoped for, bringing Lazarus back to life on the resurrection day; little did they know that You would restore him several days after he had died. Like Martha and Mary, You have given me so much more than I could ever have dared ask for. So much so, that sometimes I don't recognize that what You have given me is a gift that I've asked for, tied up in a different box and the contents are far greater than I anticipated. And even more amazing, You still give me these things after I criticize You and tell You that I don't think You know what You're doing, the same way Martha and Mary criticized You for taking too long.

At the same time, I admire Martha's faith in You to believe that You would and could bring new life to her dead brother, although she expected You to do it on Judgment Day! Praise and thanksgiving belong to You, Who not only will raise me from the dead to live in eternity with You, but also give me new life in You to make my days on earth a little bit of heaven!

JOHN 11:30-37

PRAISE JESUS WHO MOURNS WHEN I DO

Thank You, Jesus, for Your compassionate heart and for weeping at my sad heart. You know that You have the situation under control and will cause all to glorify Your name. Yes, You are such a compassionate God who shares my tears of grief and sorrow; You are not a ruthless God who puts me in certain situations and enjoys seeing me squirm. Thank You for being the kind of God who can take it when I throw tantrums and criticize You when I think You don't know what You are doing, as Mary and the Jews did when they complained about the death of Lazarus. In spite of my complaints, You don't run off and leave me but You are right there with Your arms wide open to comfort me in my distress and sorrow.

JOHN 11:38-44

PRAISE JESUS WHO GLORIFIED THE FATHER WITH WORKS.

I love You, Jesus, for You glorified the Father in the commanding action of faith and not in empty words; truly, You aren't one of those men of empty promises which are plentiful in this world. You took a dead man, Lazarus, and spoke life to him who was lifeless as a dried leaf in summer. You didn't have to speak Your healing for You could have thought it into existence, but You said it to Your Father so that others might believe in You and glorify Your Father in Heaven.

Teach me, dear Lord, to thank the Father the same way that You thanked Him. Not as a manipulative trick but as a believing and trusting child that no prayer request is too big for You. Help me also to reverence Your Holy and Precious Name whenever I ask anything, instead of coming to You half-heartedly, forgetting the God You truly are!

JOHN 11:45-46

PRAISE OR CRITICIZE

May I always come to others with high praises in my mouth for You, Lord, as some of the Jews came to Mary, excited about seeing You raise Lazarus from the dead! Let me meditate on Your Greatness and may my enthusiasm for You be of encouragement to the rest of my brothers and sisters. Forgive me, Lord, for the times I criticize You and put You down in front of others, like the Jews, who came to the Pharisees not to praise your actions but to criticize and complain. Oh my Lord, forgive me for this my unbelief, just let me praise You all the time!

Thank You, Holy Spirit, for the Revelation prophecy that You gave the High Priest, Caiaphas, that You, Jesus, would die for others so that the whole nation should not perish. What a humorous surprise for Caiaphas to come up with a Messianic prophecy, totally unexpected to the rest of the high priests and Pharisees and maybe even himself. Let my heart be open, like Caiaphas, to receive new things from You, Lord, even though they maybe unexpected and strange. Thank you, Holy Spirit, for the revelation prophecy that You gave the High Priest, Caiaphas, that You, Jesus would die for others so that the whole nation should not perish. What a humorous surprise for Caiaphas to come up with a Messianic prophecy totally unexpected to the rest of the High Priests and Pharisees and maybe even to himself! Let my heart be open, like Caiaphas to receive new things from You, Lord, even though they may be unexpected and surprising!

JOHN 11:47-55

PRAISE GOD FOR THE INSPIRED WORD

I give all praise and thanksgiving to Your Name for the things in my life that I don't think are Your will; You surprise me by turning them into greater blessings than I could ever imagine.

JOHN 11:54-57

PRAISE JESUS IN STOPPING THE PUBLIC MINISTRY

How sad it must have been for You to stop Your public ministry. You had healed the broken hearted and the physically disabled, as well as making Your Father's will known to the people, even though the chief priest and the Pharisees wanted to kill You! I remember how disappointed I felt when a friend had to stop his ministry of visiting people at a convalescent hospital where I lived, simply because one patient had a disagreement with him. My friend was also sad he had to stop seeing those he came to love there.

I also can sense the emotions You must have had in stopping Your public ministry. I was forced by two unbelievers to quit writing about You, Lord, in a monthly bulletin I sent to the public. My heart was sad because I couldn't share the joy I had in you, much as You may have felt not being able to share with the world the joy and the ways of Your Holy Father. But all praise be to You, Jesus, because no death threats or evil gossip from your countrymen against returning to Jerusalem for the Passover could stop Your ministry. You went on to die on the cross for my sins and to rise again from the dead so that I might be raised from the grave at Your Second Coming. You heal me from all my hurts and diseases; for this, I exalt and praise Your Name forever!

chapter twelve

Praise Jesus for the Privilege Of Service

JOHN 12:1-8

PRAISE YOU FOR ALLOWING ME TO GIVE YOU MY BEST

How I wish I could have been Mary so that I could have seen you in person face to face, and to have anointed Your feet with the most costly perfume; to give You all I have! Let me never (as Judas did) think that poor people could benefit from what I give. No, may it never be! For it is when I learn to take on the needs of others by taking Your heart of love and compassion that I am fulfilled. Lord, I praise You; it does my heart good when my enemies criticize me for giving to You all that I have. You are there at my defense, saying: "let him alone", as you did about Mary when she was criticized for ministering to You!

JOHN 12:9-11

PRAISE YOU FOR YOUR SAKE ALONE NOT OUT OF CURIOSITY
(PERSONAL VIEWPOINT)

Lord Jesus, let me bring all glory and praise to You, for Your Name's sake, for being the Son of the Living God! I have not come to You for curiosity sake to see Your Miracles. Thank You, Lord, for bringing to my mind a little of how You must have felt when people came to You only for the sake of Your miracle-working power, and not to seek after Your Heart.

People marvel at what I can do, communicating on my talk board, typing and oil painting in spite of my severe physical disability. They rarely look beyond the novelty of my gadgets to look into my heart. Sometimes I wish I could take all my gadgets and make my disability vanish, so that they could see the real me - the way You must have felt Lord, when everybody came to see what wonders You would perform! But I am different. Most people are kind to me, but You, my Lord, they tried to kill!

JOHN 12:12-19

HOSANNA!!!

Hosanna in the highest! Sing praise to the Lord of Lords and King of Kings! "Hosanna! Save now" were the cries of the multitude who thought that You would deliver their nation. I cry out praises to You and shout Hosannas when I think You are going to work out a particular problem in my life in a certain way, only to discover that You use different plans to solve the problem. Then my praises and my Hosannas become complaints the same way the multitude cursed and crucified You a few days after they hailed You.

Lord, forgive me for this double standard. Help me to praise You in the midst of hardship when I don't see what Your will is. Help me to trust You no matter what the outcome, in hardship as well as in times of great blessings! Humble me, Lord. I see that You made Your triumphal entry on a donkey instead of a glamorous chariot to both fulfill the prophecy in the Old Testament; becoming a humble servant. And yet for this the Pharisees sought to kill You; but you went to the cross with great Love to die for their haughty sins and mine. Praise You, Jesus!

JOHN 12:20-26

PRAISE JESUS FOR NEW LIFE

My heart does bless and magnify You, Jesus, for the new life I have. Thank You Lord for dying on the cross so that I might have eternal life and in return bear fruit. I praise You, for Your willingness to die that I might have new life; likewise, may I die to myself so that I might bear more fruit. This earthly life is often tough, but it is all worthwhile. I live for You and Your Holiness. I've fallen deeper and deeper in love with You. Lord, may I learn what it is to serve You. By Your example I want to be a servant to You and Your Father, knowing that at the end of this life on earth You will honor me for my faithfulness. I can hardly wait to hear Your words: "Well done, thou good and faithful servant!"

JOHN 12:27-43

PRAISE JESUS FOR HIS COMMITMENT TO THE FATHER UNTO DEATH

Jesus, my beautiful Savior, I give all praise and thanks to You, for Your deep commitment to humanity, for following Your Father's plan to die for me a most agonizing death! I don't know how I am going to end this mortal life, though I hope I will go quickly and painlessly.   I have no guarantee that I won't linger crying out in pain for years and years.   But You, Jesus, knew that You were going to die and that it was going to be a most painful death.   Because, for this purpose, Your Father sent You here. Your Mortal flesh cried out; You remained faithful to Your Father and glorified His Name by dying.

Cause me to hear Your Father's voice and to remember that it was for my sake You suffered and died; You could have enjoyed unbroken fellowship with Your Father.   Instead You chose to take on our mortality and human frailties to bring us to You, thereby choosing to go through Hell!   Yet in spite of what You did for me, the agony and the suffering, I still sometimes reject You to win approval of men, but the incredible thing is that You love me anyway!

JOHN 12:44-50

PRAISE TO THE FATHER WHO SENT JESUS

My heart sings sweet melodies to You, Jesus, for being the mirror reflection of Your Most Holy Father, for the confidence I have that believing in You is believing in Your Father, who is the highest good for my life.   I behold Your Father's beauty through You, Sweet Jesus; You are the light generated by Your Father to illuminate this dark world and my sinking and dying soul! Help me never to think what the unredeemed think of You; that You came as a harsh judge.   No! You came to save and redeem me from all my sin and unrighteousness.

May I tell others who don't believe Jesus, that rejecting You and Your Word is the same as a rejection of clemency. Help me to come to you daily, my Jesus, You who offers clemency for my wrong doing against Your heavenly Father.   So, my good and wonderful Lord, I thank You for the clemency that You have given me and for the commandment of Eternal Life that You drew up for me, even before the foundations of the world; Praise You, Lord!

chapter thirteen

Praise for Jesus Forgiving Heart

JOHN 13:1-31

PRAISE JESUS FOR BEING LOVE

Lord Jesus, Your love is incredible; You humbled yourself to wash Your disciples feet, even the feet of Judas Iscariot, who You knew would betray You. How awesome is Your Love, and Your knowledge. There are times in my life when I also betray You but You still love me and are ready to wash my feet! In my flesh there are times when I want to give up and quit when I see people are taking advantage of me, but You, Jesus, served the people to the very end. Lord, make me more like You to be a humble and willing servant, no matter how much it costs or how much I am rejected.

JOHN 13:4-11

PRAISE JESUS FOR BEING ABLE TO WORK IN PETER'S LIFE ,AS WELL AS, MINE

O Lord, You cause my soul to rejoice. You were so patient with individuals like Peter, who was so much like me. Sometimes I think that I don't need to have You, the Son of the very High God, serve me and wash my feet. My mind doesn't comprehend how the God who made the heavens and earth can be interested in my life and to clean all the junk away. I can take a false and pious attitude, as Peter did, thinking I can clean the junk from my life and that You don't have to bother with me. But You come and say that if I don't accept Your cleaning I will have no fellowship with You. In order for You to minister to me, I must humble myself. And like Peter, my soul so longs to be in Your Perfect Fellowship that I would want to be washed from head to feet! But, no, You have already washed me thoroughly; praise Your great and glorious Name! You need to wash the world's dust off my feet every day.

JOHN 13:12-20

PRAISE JESUS FOR BEING A LIVING EXAMPLE

O Lord, my Lord! My soul exalts the most Precious Name of Jesus, who magnifies and glorifies the Holy Father and who is a living example of praise offerings from a servant's heart. Jesus, I confess You to be the Teacher and Lord of my life. Let me be a ready and willing student of Your Ways and Statutes; may they be the dominating factor over every decision and situation I face. Thank You, Jesus, for being my Teacher, and still wanting to wash my feet; there are few teachers who are dedicated and unafraid to get involved actively in every aspect of a child's life. My favorite high-school teacher got involved with my personal life, but set a limit on her participation. But You don't place any limitations; You go all the way with me.

Thank you, Lord for giving me an example in serving others and ministering to their needs, no matter what their position in life or how they treat me. Help me to love my cantankerous Christian brothers and sisters, and unbelievers who take advantage of me and spitefully use me. Give me eyes to see that You love everyone without partiality and that You desire me to do the same. For when I love others as I love myself, I am truly blessed by You with an over-whelming joy and peace that You alone can give. For what can I say if I don't love everyone. You loved Judas Iscariot whom the scriptures tell us betrayed You! So shouldn't I receive and welcome whoever You send my way, no matter how good or bad they may be? Give me a pure heart to receive and accept anyone. You said that if I accept and welcome the outcasts as I receive my best friends I would rejoice in the joy of knowing You, King Jesus, and Your Father, whose Majesty is enthroned in Heaven!

JOHN 13:21-30

PRAISE JESUS FOR BEARING THE BETRAYAL

Lord, You comfort my soul, knowing that You had the same human feelings that I have experienced! You felt the hurt and were troubled in Your Spirit when You knew that one of Your disciples would betray and reject You. You must have felt more depressed than I did when my best friend left and abandoned me, for You knew beforehand that Judas Iscariot would be a false friend, but You loved him anyway, so much that You gave him a morsel of bread. That was a custom in that day to show a special friendship; that's real love! It would have happened in my natural flesh, I would have become very angry! I also would have told my disciples to execute vengeance on the one who betrayed me! Instead, You kept the betrayer anonymous and accepted our disciples' ignorance rather than taking vengeance on him as I would have done.

Lord, give me Your love and mercy for my betrayers and false friends, the same as You have loved and had mercy upon me for all the times that I have betrayed and hurt You. I also praise You that You gave Satan little time to do his work, for his dominion is only for a season, but Yours is forever and forever!

JOHN 13:31-35

PRAISE JESUS FOR THE MEMORIAL OF LOVE

I praise and thank You, Jesus, for being glorified in Your Father, so that His purpose might be glorified. Thank You for leaving behind a memorial, giving a new commandment to love one another, just as You love everyone in the world. No one else but You has left a memorial more precious than the commandment to love everyone as You loved me. There is no greater joy in my life than to have and to experience Your Love that is so sweet, soft, tender, and comforting and to be able to give that love to others. Lord, never let this quality of love grow cold in my life. I am now marked as one of Your Disciples; praise You for Your Love!

JOHN 13:36-38

PRAISE JESUS FOR KNOWING MY FRAILTIES

I love and adore You, dear Jesus, for knowing and accepting me just as I am, in spite of my many frailties, such as being overly self-confident, being extremely slow to grasp what You are saying. Like Simon Peter, I am sure I hear You saying something totally opposite of what You intended. You wait patiently, sometime for months or even years, until I finally get to the point where I am willing to listen to You again. You remove all my self-confidence until I am ready to completely rely on You alone. If You have to, Lord, humble me like You did with Peter, in spoiling his confidence. I need Your Holy Spirit to lead me every inch of the way on my journey, or I will surely stumble.

chapter fourteen

Praise Jesus FOR His Comfort

JOHN 14:1-4

PRAISE JESUS FOR ASSURING MY HEAVENLY HOME

I offer up my delight in You, Lord Jesus, for such comforting and assuring words, not to be troubled or afraid, but to believe and trust in You. Thank You, Jesus, for going to Your Father's house in Heaven to prepare room for me with more beautiful and elegant mansions than I could never imagine. No matter how bad things get in my life I will lift up my head and remember this promise of my heavenly home where there will be no more death and diseases, no more wheelchairs in which to confine me, no more physical barriers to overcome. I praise You also for Your promise that You are coming back to receive me unto Yourself. What a privilege to experience the fullness of Your Presence, in my new and glorified body, to be able to praise you the way I have always longed to.

JOHN 14:5-7

PRAISE JESUS FOR BEING THE WAY, THE TRUTH, AND THE LIFE.

My soul rejoices at Your marvelous character, Lord Jesus; at Your ability to answer the questions of Thomas. They were very similar to those that I would have asked of you if You had said that You were leaving me. You are the only way to the Father. Oh Lord, guide and lead me on the narrow road, as I strive to know and do Your Will. You are the truth, truer than any scientific absolute; may I always seek after Your truth which sets me free with such reality and certainty. Behold, You are the source of all truth!

You are the life of my soul that will never die. You bring life to me, truly making something out of nothing. I praise You, Jesus, who washed my sins away. You stand between the Father and me so that I am accepted by the Father. But the Father isn't some foreign God; You and Your Father are the same, why then should I be afraid? If You, Jesus, are my best friend, Your father is also my best friend, as well as my Father. Far better than any natural father. May I praise You, Jesus, forevermore for being the way to the Father, that I might come boldly before You, the essence of truth and life, to receive Your Grace and Mercy!

JOHN 14:8-11

PRAISE JESUS FOR YOUR PATIENCE

I praise You, Jesus, for being so patient with me as with Philip and the rest of Your disciples, as You tell me about something You desire me to learn; telling me over and over again until I get it straight. You never give up on me in spite of the numerous times that I disappoint You; You give me another chance to learn how to put my trust in You. You want me to know You better and better. You stretch my faith to totally rely on You even when it seems so strange and foreign to me. Your desire for me is to get so personally acquainted with You that I may know and believe in Your Father equally. You go to extremes in proving that You are in Your Father and that Your father is in You, by doing miracles that I can see every day.

JOHN 14:12-14

PRAISE JESUS FOR THE POWER OF BELIEF

O Most Holy God, You are so awesome; creating the earth and everything therein and being the true source of love, peace, and joy. You have given me and other believers the power and the ability to do greater works than Yours, that is to tell the whole world of Your Salvation Plan. Thank You, Lord Jesus, for the victory and the assurance that whatever I ask in Your Holy and Precious Name will be granted unto me as long as I walk beside You and listen to Your voice. Lord, Jesus, cause me to respect and reverence Your Holy Name, not as some empty saying at the end of a prayer but as the final authority to accomplish things that I think are humanly impossible.

JOHN 14:15-26

PRAISE JESUS FOR SENDING THE COMFORTER

Oh, how I love You, my Jesus! I adore and praise Your Holy Name. I desire with all my heart to keep Your commandment to love others as You loved and died for them. You, Lord, knew that no matter how good my intentions were that my own natural flesh couldn't love as You do, so You asked Your Father to send The Beloved Holy Spirit to be my teacher, comforter and companion. Thank You, Jesus, for not abandoning me but for giving me Your Spirit of Truth. Thank You, Lord, for sending your Holy Spirit so that You, Jesus, can live and abide in all believers any time any place.

You are my best friend; You will never leave or disappoint me. I had a close friend in grammar school who I thought would remain forever. His parents enrolled him in another school, and my little world shattered. Unlike any friend, or priest, or pope, I can come to know and love You, to praise and worship Your Father who abides in me so that I can delight in Your will and please You, Almighty King. I praise You, Holy Spirit, for constantly teaching me Your Ways for bringing to my mind Your glory Jesus, and that of Your Father.

JOHN 14:27-31

PRAISE JESUS FOR YOUR PEACE

Let my soul be quieted, O, Lord; let me be still and unconcerned about worldly matters, let my mind and heart enjoy the sweet peace that You alone can give! I praise You, Lord, for You have given me Your peace which the world cannot understand. I know that I can face anything, knowing full well that my security is in You. With Your sweet and gentle peace, I can face all of my tomorrows with a smile and full assurance that You honestly love me. Even though I may be in a wheelchair for the rest of my life with calamities befalling me right and left, and all my friends may leave me, I rejoice at the peace You freely give me! Not so with the peace that the world tries to give. They say "love and peace", but deep inside they breathe hatred because they are hurting so badly.

I am neither troubled nor fearful, because my soul is anchored in You Jesus. You abide in Your Father, who made the foundations of the earth. I rejoice in Your Love which causes my heart to believe in the eternal in spite of the darkness that the Devil tries to inflict. The prince of this world can't remotely compare with You or with what You have given me. So let my soul arise and walk in all Your ways. Just as you, Jesus, walk with the Father even unto death.

chapter fifteen

Praise Jesus FOR Making Me A Fruit Bearer

JOHN 15:1-9

PRAISE JESUS FOR PRUNING ME

All praise and glory be to Your Name, Jesus, for being the true vine and to Your Father for being the vinedresser; thank You for including me in Your branches. How humble and privileged I am to be one of Your branches. Hopefully others can see and be drawn to the You in me. Help me to be a good representative, Lord, by bearing good fruit; take the bad fruit from my life. Prune me and make me clean until I am more and more like You, dear Lord.

Thank You for Your Word, that washes me clean and acceptable before Your Father, for by Your Word I am healed from all sin and disease. Therefore, with the rich security of Your Promised Word, I came boldly into Your Grace to abide and bask in the fullness of Your wonderful Presence. If there be any sin in my life, a worthless branch in my relationship with You, convict me of it and by the power of Your Holy Spirit help me to prune what is not pleasing in Your Sight. I want to be a true and pure branch full of every good fruit by being rooted in the one and only true vine, the Lord Jesus Christ. May I so abide in You and get so close to You that I might ask for the right things which please and glorify You Father. And in my asking, may I have the proper attitude that reflects my discipleship. My security is in knowing that You and Your Father are so much in love with Me.

JOHN 15:9-17

PRAISE JESUS FOR YOUR PERFECT LOVE

Amazing love! May I always see Your Love, Lord Jesus, which Your Father first showed in its purest form. As a new-born baby is comforted in his mother's arms, may I be as comforted in Your wonderful Presence! May I forever keep Your Commandments that I can abide in You and Your perfect Law of Love, the same love that the Father showed You at the foundation of the world. Only when I scope the depth of Your Love is my joy made full, knowing that You love and accept me like nobody else can or ever will.

Yes, my joy is complete in You, realizing when I go to bed at night You are there in control of my life, for You are the One who flung the universe together! Empower me by Your Holy Spirit to capture this love that I can give it to others no matter how they treat me. Teach me that Your love for me is so intense that You laid down Your life for my sake and You call me Your Friend. "My Friend" You call me, not as a servant or a slave. You aren't distant from me. You want me to get acquainted with Your Ways; so much so, that I may come to imitate You more and more in my Christian walk.

Never allow me to take the attitude that I chose You, for You chose me – a poor miserable sinner. You turned this wretched sinner into something beautiful, even a saint, into one that brings good fruit, into one that brings other sinners to You by sharing

Your Love. Praise You, Lord Jesus, for giving me Your fruit and knowledge so that I can ask anything according to Your will and you will grant it to me. And may I always do what You command and love others as You love them.

JOHN 15:18-25

PRAISE JESUS THAT THE WORLD HATES ME

Help me to sing praises onto You, Lord, even in the midst of great trials; amidst those who would say every false and evil thing about me because I believe and testify of You. Let me be so secure in You and in Your Love that I don't care if the world hates me. May I realize that being a Christian and walking with You is not all fun and games but that I am going to be hated by those who hate You; who don't know Your incomprehensible Love. May I realize, also, that their hatred and persecution against me is really against Your Father who reveals and convicts them of their sinful nature. They don't know how beautiful You and your Father are; they just see their sins and haven't found the beauty of Your Forgiveness because of their constant rebellion against You. Thank You, Lord Jesus, for reminding me that their hatred for me is truly hatred towards You because they see You in me.

Even so, my dear Jesus, cause them to see more of You and hate me all the more even if it means damaging to my pride, or physical injury, or being martyred like many in Russia and other foreign countries. Remind me, Lord, that we are in this together and that You will never abandon me amidst their hot displeasure. Remind me that I, as Your servant, am no greater than You. Thus when people hate me for my Christian stance, I am in good company. They hated You without cause; you unveiled the darkness of their sins and pointed them to the light as their only way of escape.

JOHN 15:26-27

PRAISE JESUS FOR SENDING THE HOLY SPIRIT TO TESTIFY OF HIMSELF

My soul sings praises to You, Jesus, for sending Your Helper in the form of the Holy Spirit, even the Spirit of Truth to testify of You. I give thanks to You, Father, the essence of all truth. Even before the foundations of the world this Spirit of Truth revealed Your Father to me and assured me that You care for me. You revealed this truth to my heart from the very beginning as You revealed Yourself in all Your Glory and Power to Your Disciples.

chapter sixteen

Praise God FOR His Reassuring Comfort

JOHN 16:1-6

PRAISE JESUS FOR MAKING ME HANG ON IN THERE

Lord, help me to praise Your most Precious Name in all circumstances. You warned me that it won't be pleasant, but to be
with You is all I really need. Though some of my friends forsake
me and some so-called churches try to excommunicate me because of my fervent love and adoration, You are my friend forever,
and You will comfort me in my despair. Thank You for Your
warnings. You warned me not to stumble but to walk on with
You. Help me to realize that those who persecute me do not have
love in their hearts for You or Your Father; neither do they know
You. Thank You, Lord, for revealing this by the Power of Your
Holy Spirit. Never let my soul wait in sorrow, let me place my
hope in You.

JOHN 16:7-15

PRAISE JESUS FOR SENDING THE SPIRIT OF TRUTH

My heart and soul adore You, Lord Jesus, for giving the Helper, the Holy Spirit, to convict the world of sin and unrighteousness. I praise You that You had to go away to enable the Holy Spirit to come down to us here on earth, so that You could convict and minister not only to me, but to all the billions of people who have lived on earth. Yes, You convicted me of sin. Truly the foremost sin is not believing in You. You took my unbelief and turned it into a love affair with You! You took my filthiness and went to the cross where Your Father no longer beheld You so that I could become righteous and beautiful in Your Father's sight. You saved me from eternal damnation prepared for the Devil, and his angels, along with a company of unbelievers at Judgment day. Even now, I have victory in You. You triumphed over Satan and I am free from his doom.

Thank You, my sweet Jesus, for sending me Your Holy Spirit, the Spirit of Truth. I don't have to be concerned about my worthlessness. You take the darkness deep inside me and by the power of the Holy Spirit You turned it around to help me praise and glorify You. Thank You for the awesomeness of the Holy Spirit, who speaks of You and gives glory to You. May I always ride the crest of Your Holy Spirit, like riding the surf onto the beautiful shore; to glorify and praise Your Precious Name. I praise the Father, who certainly knows how to give good gifts.

JOHN 16:16-24

PRAISE JESUS FOR BRINGING VICTORY OUT OF DEFEAT

Jesus, my precious Jesus, You are like the sun bursting through the dark and ominous clouds bringing forth another bright, sunny day! As You tried to explain to Your disciples, You would be for a little while when you went to the pit of hell and experienced its agony and torture; Your body still in an human state was a flame of fire that would not go out no matter how You cried for mercy! You tried to explain that even the gates of hell could not hold You, and after three days of the hellish experience they would see You again as their Savior and friend! You tried to tell them that You had to ascend to Your Father in Heaven, so that I could behold Your beauty and receive Your Holy Spirit.

You are so wonderful, Jesus; You know and welcome my countless questions about You, long before I ask, You know all my thoughts! Thank You for the illustration of the mother in labor; true rejoicing breaks forth out of great pain and sorrow. So I will be glad and rejoice always! You took the agony of hell so I could be with Your Father and ask anything according to Your Will. May I realize that You truly want my life to be full and care-free; that's why you suffered and died.

JOHN 16:25-29
PRAISE JESUS FOR KNOWING THE LOVE IN MY HEART

I love You, Jesus, for speaking to me ever so gently in the beginning so as to not frighten me away. I give praise to Your Name simply because You know that I love You from the bottom of my heart. I had a friend whom I loved very much but like all imperfect people, I did something to displease her and she said that I didn't really love her. But You are different, Lord; You know that I love You deeply in spite of my sinful nature and fully knowing that I am going to sin against You. My heart rejoices in Your Love that is unconditional. Help me to not take advantage of Your Love. I give honor and glory to You for the power and the victory that I have in Your Name; everything that is asked in Your Name, Your Father will do!

JOHN 16:30-33

PRAISE YOU JESUS
THAT YOU ARE NOT DEPENDENT ON ME

I thank You that You know there will be times when I will wander and be scattered from Your Presence. I am grateful that You love me when I stop loving You; You aren't dependent upon my love. But in these times, You aren't alone, You are with Your Father interceding on my behalf. When I stray from You, dear Lord, You overcome the darkness of this world that I may come running back to You in whom I have peace again by taking my refuge in You.

chapter seventeen

Praise Jesus FOR Coming TO THE Father IN Prayer

JOHN 17:1-5

PRAISE JESUS THAT THE FATHER MAY BE GLORIFIED

Lord Jesus, I sit in amazement as You pray, communing with Your Father, God of the Most High! You, Son of the all powerful, Living God, were so close to Your Father, even from the creation of the world that You knew the Master Plan. You lifted Your eyes up and prayed to Your Father that You may glorify Him. Shouldn't I then be all the more committed to a life of prayer? You did not ask the Father for anything but to be glorified from an earthly to heavenly state, so that Your Father could also be glorified. May my prayers also be to glorify You; not asking for the things of this world that I desire. Your Father indeed glorified You by giving You authority and power over all mankind granting them eternal life. I praise You for eternal life; may I simply meditate on this gift: a life of knowing and comprehending the goodness and love of Your Father.

Being in this mortal state, I see in the mirror dimly Your Godly attributes, but when I put on my immortal body I will see clearly Your character, I will never tire of it. You glorified Your Father by Your earthly ministry demonstrating Your Father's Love and compassion and performing miraculous signs and wonders. You brought glory to Your Father, bringing together: glory, honor and majesty, even before the beginning of the world! I always praise You for Your Glory. May I please You by glorifying Your Name in whatever I do.

JOHN 17:6-19

PRAISE YOU JESUS, FOR PRAYING FOR YOUR DISCIPLES

Lord, I give you humble praise and admiration for lovingly praying for Your disciples and for committing them to Your Father's care. To them, Lord, you manifested and revealed Your true Godly nature, for which Your people had waited since the days of Abraham. Thank You for being the very best teacher that the world has ever known. You taught Your Disciples to be like God by being with them twenty four hours a day, for three and a half years. You committed their welfare and care to Your Father. Help me to do the same by committing my loved ones to You and Your Father instead of needlessly worrying about them. Yes, on my own, I surely mess things up, but when Your Hands are on a person or a situation You do it in such a way it glorifies Your Father as You did by giving Your Disciples' care to Him.

Thank You for giving your precious Word to them and for keeping Your Word in their hearts so that they would discover and tell other generations the breadth, length, height, and depth of Your Great and Marvelous Love. You sent them into the world but You did not leave them to fend for themselves in overcoming the evil one; You gave them Your spirit of Joy that would conquer all foes and make Your church alive! You knew the world would hate Your Disciples because of their joy in You. You knew no matter how much they were hated, with beatings, stoning, imprisonment, that Your joy in Your very Presence would see them through their darkest hour and usher them into the light of eternity! I thank you for Your infinite wisdom in keeping them in this world instead of secluding them in an isolated place. You commissioned them into this filthy world. You asked Your Holy Father to sanctify them and to make them holy even as You are holy and to set them apart from the rest. I offer up praise to You, Lord, for indeed cleansing them with Your Truth so I could know that You are the only True God. And so I give thanksgiving for sending them into the world accompanied by Your Truth and Joy. You weren't an over-protective parent. You gave them Your Joy and assurance that You would surely be with them in their trials and hardships.

JOHN 17:20-24

PRAISE JESUS FOR PRAYING FOR ME

I praise You, Jesus, for ministering Your Word through the work of Your Disciples who wrote the New Testament. It is awesome to meditate on the fact that You not only prayed for Your Disciples but for me as well; among the sea of people You have created over thousands of years! Let me take hold of Your Prayer that I should be one and united with all my brothers and sisters in Your Name even as You and Your Father are knit together in unity. In striving for unity with my brothers and sisters, let me see You in Your Father and Your Father in You and how You willingly followed through with Your Plan to be slaughtered like a lamb in order that I could go to heaven.

Never allow me to be content until I truly learn to love my brothers and sisters as You loved Your Father so that I may bring glory and Honor to Your Name. I remember feeling this kind of love a couple of times at camps where everyone loved each other and hugged all week long. In spite of our inadequacies, the whole week was a glory to You. But when I went down the mountain this loving and caring for people stopped. How I wish I could keep this love flowing; it brings such glory to Your Name! So I thank You, Jesus, for living through Your Disciples so that I could fall in love with You and abide in Your Presence.

JOHN 17:25-26

MISSION ACCOMPLISHED!

May I say a simple "I love You, Jesus" for calling Your Father Righteous. None other on earth above it or under it is righteous like Your Father! Thank You, Jesus, for having the most intimate fellowship with Your Father when the world could have cared less. When they saw the love You had for each other they wanted to know You and received Your Love. I offer my praise and thanksgiving for your finished work in making Your Father's name and will known to me and to others so that I could feel the love that Your Father gave to You.

chapter eighteen

Praise Jesus for Coming to the Father in Prayer

JOHN 18:1-11

PRAISE JESUS FOR HIS CLOSE FRIENDSHIP

I praise You, Jesus, and I am amazed at the way that you dealt with Judas' and Peter's situation. In my natural flesh, I would have acted much differently, completely opposite. If I were you, Jesus, I would have let Peter continue his rage, because Judas who betrayed You, told the soldiers where to arrest You. I would have allowed Peter to defend me, no matter how much it cost. But You, Lord, rebuked Peter's hot and heavy anger and went on to drink the cup Your Father gave You; You died for the sins of Judas. Lord, when my enemies do me wrong, no matter what they do, let me be like You and not allow my friends to take up my defense. Forgive me for the times I've allowed my friends to take up my defense when I could have showed Your love. May I become more like You!

JOHN 18:12-23

PRAISE JESUS FOR BEING BOUND AND HUMILIATED

I give all praise to You, King Jesus, for being arrested and bound in heavy chains like a common criminal. Worse yet the arrest orders came from Jewish officials. You were taken to Annas, father-in-law of Caiaphas the high priest. These were mere men ordained by You, the High Priest and King forever! What are mere men that You are mindful of them? You were willing to be humiliated by Your own creation!

JOHN 18:23-27

PRAISE JESUS FOR BEING DENIED

My heart gives praise and thanksgiving to You, Lord, for being the Christ and the Savior of my soul even when I, like Peter, try to deny that I ever associated with You, especially when I am asked to risk my life or social position in defending my faith. Yes, despite Peter's denial of you and sometimes mine also, You keep loving and are willing to be humiliated and beaten in the face by men who think they are higher than You. Instead, Lord let my life reflect Your Glory and testify to Your Greatness when others ask.

JOHN 18:28-32

PRAISE JESUS FOR BEING JUST TO PILATE

Jesus, You were innocent of all charges laid against You and Pontius Pilate didn't know how to deal with It. Pilate had no qualms about You, Jesus, and suspected that You had done no wrong but the Jews wanted him to commit you to them so they could kill You, the Son of the Living God. How many times have I been like Pilate; tested and seen that You are a good and loving

God, but then to bow under the pressure to make wrong judgments about You so that I would be more popular in the sight of men. Lord Jesus, forgive me for bowing under pressure, forsaking you in the midst of so-called friends or others whom I want to respect me. Lord, how many times have you forgiven me for this very thing? You died for the ways of Pilate. You also died for my sins and the errors of my ways. Help me by the power of Your Holy Spirit not to take advantage of Your forgiving nature by continuously sinning without repentance; give me boldness to speak Your Name. Praise You, Lord Jesus!

JOHN 18:33-40

PRAISE JESUS IN HIS KINGDOM

I praise and give glory to You, Jesus, for establishing a spiritual kingdom not of this world as Pilate and others had assumed You would do. You could have easily established an earthly kingdom so that I could have all worldly pleasures such as a beautiful mansion and a fleet of cars at my disposal but these luxuries could not remotely compare with Your Heavenly Kingdom that satisfies my soul now and forever! Let me be spiritually minded so that I may comprehend this Heavenly Kingdom, which Pilate tried to understand. Yes, Your kingdom is not only in Heaven but it is established in my heart that I may partake of Your Blessings and see the splendor of Your Glory. Instead of coming to the living truth, Pilate listened to the crowd and released Barabbas and let the Jews take You, Jesus, to be put to the most agonizing death on earth, by crucifixion.

I too, like Pontius Pilate come short of the truth and compromise my own beliefs, but by Your Grace and knowledge of the sincerity of my heart, You know that I really love You and thus bring me into Your Kingdom. Thank You, Lord!

chapter nineteen

Praise Jesus for Going All the Way

JOHN 19:1-3

PRAISE JESUS FOR ENDURING SUFFERING AT THE HAND OF PILATE

Oh, what pain You endured Jesus, when Pontius Pilate had you scourged with a leather whip marking up Your Body. It was so bloody, that You were almost unrecognizable. What pain You must have suffered with every crack of the whip! Pilate ordered his soldiers to force a crown of sharp thorns on Your head and beat Your face until they no longer knew what You looked like.

May I meditate on these Scriptures so that I can discover the pain and agony You suffered in dying for my sins! May I never take a passive attitude reading the accounts of Your suffering. Let me feel every single lashing of the whip on Your back and every blow to Your face! Besides all the physical pain You contended with, You also had to endure the ridicule of the soldiers mocking You with shouts of "hail the King of the Jews", yet You did not say a word or lift a finger in Your defense.

JOHN 19:4—16

WHICH KING DO I SERVE?

As Pontius Pilate debated what to do with You, Lord Jesus, he allowed his decision to be swayed by his loyalty to Caesar. Likewise I am also easily swayed when others give me the choice to serve either You or other gods and kings. Forgive me Lord, for being so non-committal. Fix my heart more towards You so that they may even crucify me alongside of You!

JOHN 19:17-22

SEEING YOU CRUCIFIED

I praise You, Lord Jesus; my spirit is grieved reflecting upon the painful Crucifixion. You were labeled by the inscription Pilate put on the cross after being scourged, having a crown of thorns on Your Head and Your Face beaten to a bloody pulp. How humiliating it must have been to be crucified with nails in Your hands and feet like the thieves on each side of You. You are the King and the God of the whole world. Nevertheless, You withstood the humiliation and did not defend Yourself; You explained that You are the King the Son of the Living God. You could have called ten thousand angels to help You from the cross, but praise You Lord Jesus; You endured the crucifixion and all the humiliation to become my King and Redeemer.

JOHN 19:23-24

PRAISE JESUS FOR ENDURING SIN AND SHAME

I was reminded of the shame You must have felt when some nurses at a convalescent hospital dressed and undressed me where all could see, instead of pulling curtains for privacy. I tried to tell them to close the curtains but they didn't want to take the time to understand. At least I was inside, but You hung naked on the cross as a public spectacle for the whole world to see. After stripping You naked, the soldiers had the audacity to divide Your garments and to cast lots for them; yet You continued to love even these soldiers!

JOHN 19:25-27

MARY BEHOLDING HER SON, JESUS

What a horrifying sight it must have been for Your mother to see You, Jesus. She saw You painfully suffering and dying on the cross; You the redeemer of all mankind and King forever. As she gazed at You there, Mary must have thought back to the miraculous virgin conception; the way that she cuddled and cradled You in her arms when You were a baby. She might have remembered You saying that You must be about Your Father's business. You indeed were the Promised Messiah the fulfillment of prophecies heard since she was a child.   Like any other mother, she hated to see her son in pain and suffering, but she must have known that You must bear the pain and agony of the world to become the long awaited Messiah, Redeemer, and King.

JOHN 19:28-30

IT'S FINISHED AND COMPLETE

I praise You, Lord Jesus, for Your finished work on the cross; not a single prophecy unfulfilled! Your lovingkindness extended to all. There was nothing unfinished as You hung there on the cross six hours, with the agony, defeat and the sins of mankind on Your shoulders. With your lips parched and Your tongue clinging to Your mouth, dehydrated, exhausted and paralyzed on the cross You said You were thirsty and the soldiers added to Your Thirst by giving You some sour wine. Then the most awesome phenomena in all of history: You gave up Your spirit and died. For in giving up Your spirit, You gave up the love of Your Father which You always had enjoyed since the beginning of time.

It is hard to comprehend You losing precious fellowship with the Father, with whom You created heaven and earth. In one single moment You went on to spend three days tormented in hell with weeping and gnashing of teeth, to atone for my sin. Losing fellowship with Your Father is like a person in perfect health suddenly stricken by a debilitating disease. Cause me to remember that You love me so much that You were willing to die and suffer the horror and terror of hell itself for me!

JOHN 19:31-37

PRAISE JESUS FOR FULFILLING PROPHECY AFTER DEATH

I will bring glory to Your name, Holy Jesus, although You hung on the cross dead, completely lifeless, the Holy Spirit, continued performing miracles in fulfilling prophecy. The soldiers broke the legs of the two thieves on each side of You, Jesus, but when they came to You, You were already dead; there was no need to break Your legs, fulfilling Old Testament Prophecy. I praise You, Lord, for Your Miracle-working Power while on earth. I sit in amazement that You kept on fulfilling Scriptures by the power of the Holy Spirit.

JOHN 19:38-42

RICHES FOR JESUS

May I become like Joseph of Arimathea and Nicodemus who gave their best possessions to honor You in Your burial. Joseph gave his highly treasured tomb wherein to lay Your body. Nicodemus brought costly spices for Your burial. So because You are alive, I should give the best I have. Therefore, may I praise You with the very best I have, making melodies to You, Lord, all day long!

chapter twenty

Praise Jesus FOR THE Victory

JOHN 20:1-18

HALLELUJAH, MY JESUS IS RISEN

Hallelujah! You, my sweet Jesus, are risen. You are alive even for me today! Lord Jesus, thank You for giving me the highs and lows with a friend I thought had died, so that I could feel the emotion of Mary Magdalene and Your Disciples when they thought Your body had been stolen from he tomb, but You were alive! I thought that my good friend, Mark, had died at a near-by hospital. He had pneumonia and muscular dystrophy. All of us were crying, grieving at the loss of one we all loved and admired. His girl friend was in hysteria. But suddenly we got word some-how there was a misunderstanding between the hospital and the nursing home; Mark was still alive! After a couple of us went to the hospital to verify that, we found that, yes, it was true. All the patients and staff at the nursing home went from mourning to rejoicing, even dancing in our wheelchairs because our friend who we had known and loved for years was alive!

Mary Magdalene and Your disciples were shocked and saddened to see Your body mysteriously missing from the tomb; but much more overjoyed to see You, Jesus, alive! It must have been doubly heartbreaking for Mary to see the empty tomb; she had placed all her trust and hope in You who knew that she was a prostitute. She must have been elated beyond mere words when she found out that it was You, Jesus, who spoke to her in the garden. You were alive and well and her trust and hope burst with renewed enthusiasm. You did what You had promised and rose from the dead to prepare her a mansion in heaven forever. Her sins were forever washed away. You are alive and well today. I can put my trust and hope in You though my sins may be as Mary's. Yes, Praise You, Jesus, for being alive.

JOHN 20:19-21

PRAISE JESUS FOR YOUR PEACE

I shout thanksgiving and honor to you, most Holy Jesus, for the deep, abiding love that You give me; such a peace cancels out fear. You calmed the fears of Your Disciples assuring them that it was You, Lord, in your resurrection body, with scars on Your hands and Your side from the ordeal on the cross. Your resurrection appearance, Your reassuring words of peace, erased their fears. For now there was nothing to fear. You, Jesus, the Almighty God, would surely go with them. Even death was under Your control, for You had taken the sting out of death! Hallelujah!

Likewise through Your Resurrection Power, You give me the same soothing and comforting peace. You are with me wherever I may go, even through death! So thank You, Holy Lord, for the perfect peace You have given me. May I cherish and nourish it all the days of my life.

JOHN 20:22-23

BY YOUR HOLY SPIRIT GIVE ME DISCERNMENT

I give Glory and Honor to You, Jesus, my Living Lord, for breathing into Your disciples the infilling of Your Holy Spirit. You have given me the same authority by the power of Your Holy Spirit. Let me esteem and reverence this power that I may never abuse it by passing false judgments, because I have not taken the time to listen to Your voice, oh most Precious Holy Spirit. Cause me to remember that Your Grace abounds; yes, You died to forgive!

JOHN 20:24-29

PRAISE JESUS WHO SAYS THAT I AM BLESSED

My Lord and my God, my soul rejoices and is exhilarated in the fact that You, God, called me "blessed" just for believing You by faith without seeing You physically! You, Lord, make me leap for joy in telling Your disciple, Thomas, that I have blessings coming because I am willing to believe in You by faith, not insisting on physical evidence.

You are God, Almighty, all knowing and ever present, the maker and great designer of heavens and earth and everything therein! You are my Lord. You take such personal interest in me. You died on the cross that my sins will be remembered no more! Yes, You rose from the dead and live even today so that I will have my new glorified body, perfect in every way, and I will live eternally with You, the Great Lord and God. I give thanksgiving and all praise to You, for the gift of Your Holy Spirit Who revealed You. I believe in You by faith, and You call me blessed for believing.

JOHN 20:30-31

IF THAT ISN'T ENOUGH

O Lord, My Precious God, You are so beautiful, so very dear to my soul: You, Jesus the Christ, the Anointed One, the Promised Messiah! Thank You, my Lord Jesus, for doing miraculous signs and wonders recorded in the other gospels. You are everything You claimed to be. I put all my faith and will to believe and trust in You!

Thank You for this documentation, that not only I may believe in You, but that in Your name as the Messiah and the Son of the Living God I may have life and more abundant life here on earth and everlasting life in heaven. My heart rejoices and sings for joy for this life in You, Lord. I see a man with no hope as I see a friend on his death bed. I praise and thank You for this life of everlasting joy, for being my Jesus, My Messianic Christ, and my Precious Lord, the Son of the Almighty God!

chapter twenty-one

Praise Jesus FOR Being Worthy TO BE Followed AS THE Risen Christ

JOHN 21:1-14

PRAISE JESUS FOR TUNING ME IN

I praise and adore You, Lord, for accepting and loving me exactly as I am, as high as a mountain-top, or as deep as the valley. I thank You, Lord for bringing me to a new and thrilling experience with You replacing my apathy and discouragement with a multitude of fish on the other side of my boat. You bless me so much with the little things of life. You lift my spirits, and show me that You are still Lord! Your Disciples went fishing and were saddened, as I am, after a mountain-top experience, such as seeing You in Your Glorified Body. How many times have I been praising You one day, to feeling down-trodden and discouraged the next. The enemy, the devil, tries to rob my joy. Forgive me for these times. And how many times have you picked me up from my despair and gloom to show me in a very special way that You still love me. Like Your disciples of old, please give me enough of Your Holy Spirit to obey Your Word and receive Your blessing. Nevertheless, teach me to flee from despair and discouragement and celebrate the wonders of Your Resurrection every day and every moment of the Year. Hallelujah! You are alive. You are my Lord and My God!

JOHN 21:15-17

PRAISE JESUS FOR THE CHALLENGE OF LOVE

My dear and precious Lord, I thank You for the challenge of love, by challenging me to love as You challenged Peter, asking him if he really loved You. Love becomes an empty word until it is affirmed by action, such as tending and caring for the Lambs that You have redeemed. Lord, may I always instruct others in the love and the admonition of Your Way, not keeping Your Greatness and Graciousness for myself and my friends. Always remind me, Lord, that there are many who desperately need you and Your peace in their lives. Let me reaffirm Your Love in my life by shouting Your Goodness from the mountain tops, by sharing Your gentleness to others who need Your Salvation. Look inside my heart, as You did with Peter, to see if I really love You. If You see an emptiness in my love, prove me a little harder until I examine my love for You. Your probing and questioning may insult and offend me at first, but I would rather have a genuine love for You and become a doer of Your Word by demonstrating my love in action.

JOHN 21:18-19

PRAISE JESUS FOR BRINGING ME MATURITY

I give all praise to you, Lord, for growth. You accepted my youthful ways as a new Christian and molded me to maturity; may I become a bond servant, even a martyr. Like Peter, I was like a wild stallion making my mark as a babe in You, but You put up with my childish ways. As I grow older in You, stretch me and mold me into Your Image; I will go anywhere and anytime You want. As I love You more and more, perfect me until I surrender all to You; You are all I really need. I love You, Lord, and I lift my praises to Your Most Holy Name for maturing and refining me in Your time. Do what You want; I will truly follow You!

JOHN 21:20-23

JESUS, TEACH ME HOW TO FOLLOW YOU

I love and greatly adore You, Jesus. Please teach me how to follow You in a manner most acceptable and pleasing in Your Sight. Like Peter I tend to become preoccupied with friends who are following You when I should be more concerned about my personal walk with You. Sometimes I hear a sermon and I think the message would be beneficial to another brother or a sister or someone who needs Your Salvation but the message is really intended for me. Lord, forgive me of this presumptuous attitude. Teach me to commit these people in prayer, knowing You will speak to them when they are able to receive. Help me to listen to Your voice instruct me in Your Ways. Yes, Lord, teach me to follow You, to be concerned with my walk with You. It is when I am right with You that others will come to love Your way and will for their lives.

JOHN 21:24-25

PRAISE JESUS FOR A FULL AND A COMPLETE GOSPEL

I praise and adore You, Lord Jesus; I thank You for revealing Your Life to John so that I can read about God the King and to fall deeper in love in You! You are worthy. Your truth is worth risking my life, as was John's in his exile on the Island of Patmos. I praise you that John was an eye witness of Your Resurrection; nobody disputed this until 200 years afterwards. Only a fool would contradict an event that was seen by eye witnesses. The accounts of Your Life, as John wrote in addition to the other gospels, is only a fragment of Your accomplishments and miracles performed in your 33 years on earth. You had such a full and a rich life that all the libraries in the world could not even possibly contain the things You did, the signs and wonders, but most of all Your Love.

So please Lord Jesus, accept the meditation and the praise from my heart in reading the Gospels of Your Life knowing that my praise is like a mist of what You truly deserve! Hallelujah Jesus and Amen!

To order additional copies of

Psalms Of Praises

to the gospel of saint john

have your credit card ready and call
1 800-917-BOOK (2665)

or e-mail
orders@selahbooks.com

or order online at
www.selahbooks.com

Printed in the United States
62409LVS00004B/216

9 781589 301399